Collins

The Shanghai Maths Project

For the English National Curriculum

Series Editor: Professor Lianghuo Fan

UK Curriculum Consultant: Paul Broadbent

Practice Book 4

William Collins' dream of knowledge for all began with the publication of his first book in 1819. A self-educated mill worker, he not only enriched millions of lives, but also founded a flourishing publishing house. Today, staying true to this spirit, Collins books are packed with inspiration, innovation and practical expertise. They place you at the centre of a world of possibility and give you exactly what you need to explore it.

Collins. Freedom to teach.

Published by Collins
An imprint of HarperCollins*Publishers* Ltd.
The News Building
1 London Bridge Street
London SE 1 9GF

Browse the complete Collins catalogue at
www. collins. co. uk

© HarperCollins*Publishers* Limited 2016
© Professor Lianghuo Fan 2016
© East China Normal University Press Ltd. 2016

10 9 8 7 6 5 4 3 2 1

ISBN: 978-0-00-814465-4

The Shanghai Maths Project (for the English National Curriculum) is a collaborative effort between HarperCollins, East China Normal University Press Ltd. and Professor Lianghuo Fan and his team. Based on the latest edition of the award-wining series of learning resource books, *One Lesson One Exercise*, by East China Normal University Press Ltd. in Chinese, the series of Practice Books is published by HarperCollins after adaptation following the English National Curriculum.

Practice book Year 4 is translated and developed by Professor Lianghuo Fan with assistance of Ellen Chen, Ming Ni, Jing Xu and Dr. Jane Hui-Chuan Li, with Paul Broadbent as UK curriculum consultant.

British Library Cataloguing in Publication Data
A Catalogue record for this publication is available from the British Library.

Series Editor: Professor Lianghuo Fan
UK Curriculum Consultant: Paul Broadbent
Commissioned by Lee Newman
Project Managed by Fiona McGlade and Mike Appleton
Design by Kevin Robbins and East China Normal University Press Ltd.
Typesetting by East China Normal University Press Ltd.
Cover illustration by Daniela Geremia
Production by Rachel Weaver
Printed by Grafica Veneta S. p. A

Contents

Chapter 10 Four operations of whole numbers

Chapter 1 Revising and improving

1.1 Warm-up revision

Learning objective

Use strategies to calculate mentally and using written methods

Basic questions

1 Calculate.

$200 + 300 =$	$460 - 230 =$	$170 + 330 =$
$1000 - 400 =$	$470 - 230 =$	$660 - 600 =$
$500 + 500 =$	$480 - 230 =$	$290 + 110 =$

2 Find patterns and fill in the boxes.

$148 + 152 =$	$855 - 170 =$	$220 + 348 =$
$138 + 162 =$	$865 - 170 =$	$220 + 350 =$
$128 + 172 =$	$\boxed{} - 170 =$	$220 + 352 =$
$\boxed{} + \boxed{} =$	$885 - 170 =$	$\boxed{} + \boxed{} =$

3 Fill in the brackets.

(a) A square has (   ) sides and (   ) angles. The lengths of all the sides are (   ). All the angles are (   ) angles and equal to (   ) degrees.

(b) A cuboid has (   ) vertices, (   ) faces and (   ) edges.

(c) A cube has (   ) faces. The shape of each face is a (   ).

4 Fill in the brackets.

(a) Write a suitable unit in each bracket.

Joan's weight is about 32 (   ).   There are 24 (   ) in a day. This morning, Tom spent 10 (   ) eating a piece of bread which weighs about 100 (   ).

(b) Write a suitable number in each bracket.

1000 grams = (   ) kilogram(s)

1 hour 17 minutes = (   ) minutes

2 minutes = (   ) second(s)   35 g + 423 g = (   ) g

2012 was a leap year and it had (   ) weeks and (   ) days, or in total (   ) days.

5 Use the column method to calculate.

(a) $362 + 607 =$ (b) $1000 - 872 =$ (c) $631 - 89 + 452 =$

6 Write a suitable number in each ☐.

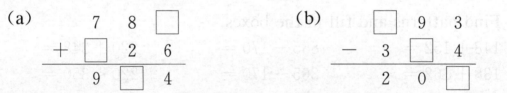

(a)
```
    7  8  □
 +  □  2  6
 ─────────
    9  □  4
```

(b)
```
    □  9  3
 −  3  □  4
 ─────────
    2  0  □
```

Challenge and extension questions

7 Think carefully and fill in the boxes with suitable numbers.

(a) $18 \times 9 + 18$

$= 18 \times \boxed{}$

$= \boxed{}$

(b) $21 \times 6 - 6$

$= \boxed{} \times \boxed{}$

$= \boxed{}$

8 Make a count. In the figure on the right, there are (   ) letter 'A's and (   ) triangles.

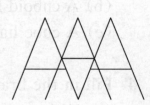

1.2 Multiplication tables up to 12 × 12

Learning objective

Recall multiplication facts and division facts

Basic questions

1 Write the multiplication facts and complete the table.

×	1	2	3	4	5	6	7	8	9	10	11	12
10	10				50					100		
11		22				66					121	
12			36				84					144

2 Use the multiplication table above to complete two multiplication sentences with the given product and write the multiplication fact. The first one has been done for you.

Product: 60

5 × 12 = 60 (or 6 × 10 = 60)

12 × 5 = 60 (or 10 × 6 = 60)

Multiplication fact:

5 × 12 = 60 (or 6 × 10 = 60)

Product: 88

_____

_____

Multiplication fact:

_____

Product: 110

_____

_____

Multiplication fact:

_____

Product: 132

_____

_____

Multiplication fact:

_____

3 Fill in the brackets.

96 = (8) × (   ) = (12) × (   ) = (6) × (   )

$44 = (4) \times (\quad) = (11) \times (\quad) = (2) \times (\quad)$

$108 = (9) \times (\quad) = (12) \times (\quad) = (3) \times (\quad)$

4 Calculate.

$12 \times 5 =$	$11 \times 6 =$	$9 \times 11 =$	$24 \div 2 =$
$5 \times 11 =$	$7 \times 11 =$	$12 \times 12 =$	$33 \div 11 =$
$11 \times 10 =$	$100 \div 10 =$	$11 = (\quad) \div 12$	$12 = (\quad) \div 6$

5 Mother Monkey collected 121 bananas and gave all of them to 11 baby monkeys equally. How many bananas did each baby monkey get?

6 Sharon reads 12 pages of a book every day. The book has 308 pages. She has read the book for 11 days. How many pages has Sharon read? How many pages are left?

Challenge and extension questions

7 A deck of cards can be counted in 11s and in 12s respectively, without any left over. What is the least possible number of the cards in the deck?

8 All pupils in Year 4 are grouped equally for a school activity. If each group consists of 10 pupils, there are 6 pupils left ungrouped. If each group consists of 11 pupils, there are 4 pupils left ungrouped. Given that the number of pupils in Year 4 is fewer than 150, how many pupils are there in Year 4?

1.3 Multiplication and division (1)

Learning objective

Multiply and divide three-digit numbers by a single digit number

Basic questions

1 Use the column method to calculate. (Check the answers to the questions marked with ∗ .)

$89 \times 6 =$ **$801 \div 9 =$ $8 \times 356 =$

$293 \times 5 =$ **$769 \div 7 =$ $464 \div 8 =$

2 Fill in the ◯ with $>$, $<$ or $=$.

$87 \div 3 \bigcirc 78 \div 3$ $150 \div 5 \bigcirc 105 \div 5$ $264 \div 4 \bigcirc 272 \div 4$

$75 \div 5 \bigcirc 75 \div 3$ $392 \div 2 \bigcirc 392 \div 8$ $756 \div 8 \bigcirc 756 \div 7$

$96 \div 8 \bigcirc 84 \div 7$ $650 \div 5 \bigcirc 990 \div 9$ $610 \div 5 \bigcirc 738 \div 6$

3 Work these out step by step.

$6 \times 187 - 216$ $585 \div 5 + 78$ $408 \times 7 + 973$

4 Jack is 8 years old. He and his younger brother, Joe, went to a theme park with their parents on a Sunday. The admission ticket was £36 for an adult and £25 for a child under 12. How much did they pay for the admission tickets in total?

5 The table below shows the information of three pupils in a running exercise. Find out who runs the fastest and who runs the slowest.

	Tom	John	James
Time (minutes)	5	8	4
Distance (metres)	675	768	544

 Challenge and extension questions

6 Mary went to buy some pens with £54. There were three prices for the pens: £9, £6 and £18 each respectively. Please help Mary find out how to choose different numbers of the pens so the total cost is exactly £54.

7 Fill in the boxes with suitable numbers to make the calculation true.

(a)

$$
\begin{array}{r}
\boxed{}\,8\,\boxed{} \\
\times \quad\quad \boxed{} \\
\hline
7\ 0\ \boxed{}\ 5
\end{array}
$$

(b)

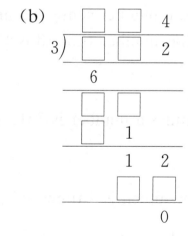

1.4 Multiplication and division (2)

Learning objective

Multiply and divide three-digit numbers by a single digit number

Basic questions

1 Use the column method to calculate.

(a) $130 \times 6 =$ (b) $620 \div 4 =$ (c) $560 \div 8 =$ (d) $537 \div 9 =$

2 Work these out step by step.

(a) $462 \times 7 + 367$ (b) $780 \times 5 - 1000$ (c) $658 + 326 - 558$

3 Write the number sentences and then calculate.

(a) What number times 8 is 1000?

(b) 7 times a number is 721. Find this number.

(c) How much is 5 times 465?

(d) The divisor is 65, the quotient is 8 and the remainder is 9. What is the dividend?

4 Application problems.

(a) A box of cola has 10 bottles. Each bottle has 380 ml. John has drunk 4 bottles. How many millilitres has he drunk? How many millilitres of cola are still left in the box?

(b) Joan's father is 40 years old this year. This is exactly 4 times Joan's age. How many years younger than her father is Joan?

(c) One lap of the running track in a school sports field is 200 metres long. Mary has run 4 laps and John has run 1 kilometre. (Note: 1 kilometre＝1000 metres or 1 km＝1000 m.)

(i) How many metres has Mary run?

(ii) How many laps has John run? How many more metres has he run than Mary?

Challenge and extension questions

5 A school bought some footballs and basketballs. There are 20 more basketballs than footballs. The number of basketballs is 3 times the number of footballs. How many footballs did the school buy? How about basketballs?

6 In the following column calculation, what numbers do A, B, C and D stand for in order to make the calculation correct?

```
      A  B  C
×           C
─────────────
      D  B  C
```

1.5 Problem solving (1)

 Learning objective

Use strategies to solve multiplication and division problems

 Basic questions

1 A school library has 48 science books. The number of storybooks is 15 more than 3 times the number of science books. How many storybooks does the library have? (Hint: refer to the line model given.)

2 Tom is 11 years old. His father is 5 years younger than 4 times Tom's age. How old is Tom's father? (Hint: draw a line model to analyse.)

3 There are 34 rabbit-shaped lanterns. The number of ball-shaped lanterns is 3 times the number of the rabbit-shaped lanterns.

(a) How many rabbit-shaped lanterns and ball-shaped lanterns are there altogether?

Method Ⅰ: Method Ⅱ:

(b) How many more ball-shaped lanterns are there than rabbit-shaped lanterns?

Method Ⅰ: Method Ⅱ:

④ John, Mary and Andy all like collecting stamps. John has collected 24 stamps. He has 8 stamps fewer than Mary. The number of stamps that Andy has collected is 3 times the number of stamps that Mary has collected. How many stamps does Andy have?

Challenge and extension questions

⑤ There are 360 willow trees in a city area. There are 10 more oak trees than twice the number of willow trees. The number of maple trees is 10 fewer than twice the number of willow trees.

(a) How many oak and maple trees are there in total?

(b) How many fewer maple trees are there than oak trees?

⑥ 865 trees are planted around a lake. Two maple trees are planted between every two willow trees. How many willow trees and maple trees are planted, respectively?

1.6   Problem solving (2)

Learning objective

Use strategies to solve multiplication and division problems

Basic questions

1 Look at the diagrams below, write the number sentences and calculate.

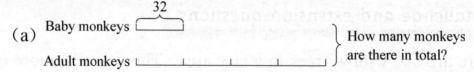

(a) Baby monkeys — 32

Adult monkeys

How many monkeys are there in total?

(b) Pens — 19

Pencils

How many?

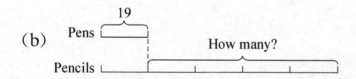

2 Write the number sentences and calculate.

(a) A is 357. B is 3 times as great as A. What is the sum of A and B?

(b) A is 357. It is 3 times as great as B. What is the sum of A and B?

3 3000 kilograms of rice were delivered to the warehouse in a morning. The amount of rice delivered in the afternoon was 2000 kilograms more than twice the amount delivered in the morning. How many kilograms of rice were delivered in the afternoon?

4 A high-speed train travels 240 kilometres in one hour. This is 4 times as fast as a car. How many more kilometres does the high-speed train travel than the car in one hour?

5 A farm has 120 cows. The number of sheep is 3 times the number of cows. The number of pigs is 5 times the number of cows.
(a) How many fewer cows than pigs are there on the farm?

(b) How many more pigs than sheep are there on the farm?

(c) How many cows, pigs and sheep are there altogether?

Challenge and extension questions

6 There were 72 pupils in the reading room and in the art room altogether. After 12 pupils left the art room and entered the reading room, there were 3 times as many pupils in the reading room as in the art room. How many pupils were there in the reading room and in the art room at first?

7 A 90 metre-long rope is cut into two parts. The first part is 2 metres shorter than 3 times the length of the second part. How long is the second part?

1.7 Fractions

Learning objective

Recognise, find and calculate fractions of shapes and quantities

Basic questions

1 Fill in the blanks with fractions.

(a) The cake was divided into two equal parts. Each part is _____ of the cake.

(b) The chocolate bar was divided into eight equal parts. Each part is _____ of the chocolate bar.

(c) The square is divided into four equal parts. Each part is _____ of the whole.

2 Use a fraction to represent the shaded part of each figure.

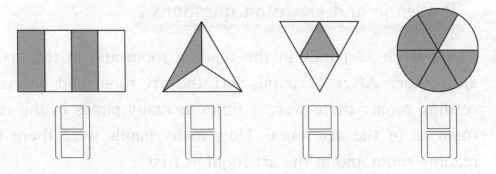

3 Colour each figure below to represent the fraction given.

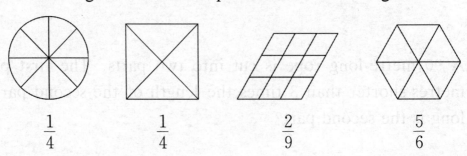

$\frac{1}{4}$ $\frac{1}{4}$ $\frac{2}{9}$ $\frac{5}{6}$

4 Circle $\frac{1}{6}$ and $\frac{2}{5}$ respectively.

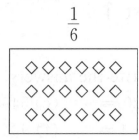

5 Fill in the blanks.

(a) $\frac{1}{2}$ of 20 ▲ is (　　) ▲.

(b) $\frac{1}{5}$ of 20 ▲ is (　　) ▲.

(c) $\frac{3}{4}$ of 20 ▲ is (　　) ▲.

Challenge and extension question

6 Use fractions to represent the shaded parts in the figures below.

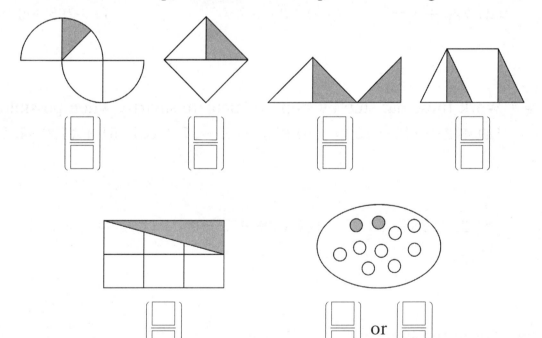

Unit test 1

1 Work these out mentally, then write the answers.

(a) $150 + 450 =$ (b) $680 - 320 =$ (c) $540 - 450 =$

(d) $12 \times 12 =$ (e) $64 \div 8 \div 4 =$ (f) $9 \times (\ ) = 27 + 9$

(g) $200 \div 50 =$ (h) $300 \div 30 =$ (i) $11 \times 12 =$

(j) $70 + (\ ) = 120$ (k) $720 \div (\ ) = 9$ (l) $(\ ) \times 8 = 80$

2 Use the column method to calculate. (Check the answers to the questions marked with $*$.)

(a) $1000 - 888 =$ (b) $987 - 789 + 123 =$ (c) $3 \times 285 =$

(d) $720 \div 4 =$ (e) $* 89 \div 7 =$ (f) $* 365 \div 9 =$

3 Work these out step by step. (Calculate smartly when possible.)

(a) $472 - 148 - 152$ (b) $213 - 43 + 87$ (c) $751 + 273 - 451$

(d) $25 \times 78 \times 4$ (e) $1008 \div 7 \div 9$ (f) $24 \times 5 + 333$

4 Fill in the brackets.

(a) Use the numbers 1, 2, 3, 4, 5, 6, 7, 8 and 9 to form two three-digit numbers. Do not use the same digit twice. The greatest possible difference between two such numbers is (   ).

16

(b) $500 \div ($ $) = 10$ $($ $) \times 7 = 4900$ $($ $) \div 8 = 30$

(c) Fill in ◯ with $>$, $<$ or $=$.

$48 \div 4$ ◯ $84 \div 4$ $219 \div 3$ ◯ $192 \div 3$ $606 \div 6$ ◯ $630 \div 6$

$360 \div 6$ ◯ $360 \div 60$ $615 \div 3$ ◯ $615 \div 5$ $428 \div 4$ ◯ $428 \div 2$

(d) Write a suitable unit in each bracket.

Tom is 120 (   ) tall.

The mass of an egg is 70 (   ).

The height of a desk is 100 (   ).

The mass of a watermelon is 4 (   ).

The Tower Bridge in London is 244 (   ) long.

A football costs 15 (   ).

John's height is 1 (   ) and 45 (   ).

A car travels at 60 (   ) per hour.

(e) A circle was divided into 6 equal parts. Each part is (   ) of the circle.

(f) 7 lots of $\dfrac{1}{(\ \ \ )}$ is equal to seven ninths.

(g) The denominator of a fraction is 34 and the numerator is 11 less than the denominator. The fraction is (   ).

(h) There are (   ) lots of $\dfrac{1}{21}$ in $\dfrac{3}{21}$.

(i) A 1-metre-long ribbon was divided into 5 equal pieces. The length of each piece is (   ). Four such pieces are (   ) metres long.

5 Colour each figure below to represent the fraction given.

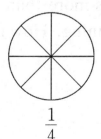

$\dfrac{1}{4}$

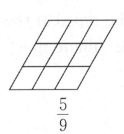

$\dfrac{5}{9}$

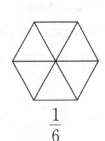

$\dfrac{1}{6}$

6 In each figure below, what fraction of it is shaded? Fill in the brackets.

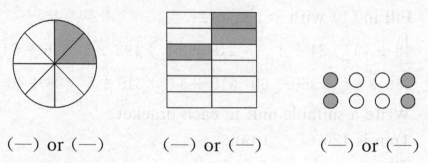

(—) or (—)   (—) or (—)   (—) or (—)

7 Application problems.

(a) Mary cut a 15-metre-long ribbon into lengths of 3 metres each. How many cuts did Mary make?

(b) Trees are planted every 4 metres along the side of a road. Joan ran from the first tree and stopped at the tenth tree. How many metres did she run?

(c) 42 pots of flowers are placed along both sides of a corridor. They are placed 3 metres apart. How long is the corridor?

(d) When Tom started learning typing, he could type 15 words in one minute. Now he can type 7 words more than 4 times the number of words he typed at the beginning. How many words can he type in one minute now?

(e) In a supermarket, a box of chocolate costs £18 and a pack of cashew nuts costs £28. The price of rice is £42 per sack. Tom and his father went shopping with £400.

(i) They first bought 2 packs of cashew nuts and 3 sacks of rice. How much did they pay?

(ii) Tom then bought 3 boxes of chocolate. How much did they pay for the chocolate?

(iii) How much money had they left?

Chapter 2　Numbers to and beyond 1000 and their calculation

2.1　Knowing numbers beyond 1000 (1)

 Learning objective

Place value of four-digit numbers

 Basic questions

1 Work these out mentally, and then write the answers.

$63 + 91 + 20 =$ 　　　$21 - 3 + 6 =$ 　　　$54 - 46 - 2 =$

$9 \times 1 \times 4 =$ 　　　$8 \times 2 \times 7 =$ 　　　$60 \div 4 \div 5 =$

$120 \div 5 \div 6 =$ 　　　$0 \times 3 \times 0 =$ 　　　$70 \div 10 \times 9 =$

$180 \div 10 \div 3 =$ 　　　$98 + 32 + 44 =$ 　　　$30 \div 10 \times 9 =$

2 Read and write the numbers given below. The first one has been done for you.

(a) The longest road distance in the United Kingdom is from Land's End to John o'Groats: 1407 km.

Read as: <u>One thousand four hundred and seven</u>

$1407 = \underline{1000} + \underline{400} + \underline{0} + \underline{7}$

(b) The highest mountain in the United Kingdom is Ben Nevis. It is located in the Scottish Highlands, and stands at 1344 m above the sea level.

Read as: _____

$1344 = \underline{\quad} + \underline{\quad} + \underline{\quad} + \underline{\quad}$

(c) The flight distance from London to New York is 5586 km.

Read as: _____

$5586 = \underline{\quad} + \underline{\quad} + \underline{\quad} + \underline{\quad}$

(d) The Great Wall of China is about 6700 km long.

Read as: _____

6700=_____+_____+_____+_____

(e) The Nile in the north-east of Africa is the longest river in the world. It is 6853 km long.

Read as: _____

6853=_____+_____+_____+_____

3 Complete the place value chart.

1001

Ten thousands	Thousands	Hundreds	Tens	Ones

9212

Ten thousands	Thousands	Hundreds	Tens	Ones

7035

Ten thousands	Thousands	Hundreds	Tens	Ones

10 535

Ten thousands	Thousands	Hundreds	Tens	Ones

4 Fill in the brackets.

(a) There are (   ) thousands and (   ) hundreds in four thousand.

(b) 5 tens make (   ). 5 hundreds make (   ). 5 thousands make (   ).

(c) From the right, the first place of a number is the (   ) place. The place to its left is the (   ) place.

(d) From the right, the fourth place of a number is the (   ) place. The place to its right is the (   ) place. The place to its left is the (   ) place.

(e) The number 4075 consists of 4 (   ), (   ) tens and 5 (   ). It reads (   ). The difference between this number and the greatest three-digit number is (   ).

⑤ Multiple choice questions.

   (a) 8 is in both the thousands place and the hundreds place. This number is (   ).

     A. 88 000   B. 8800   C. 880

   (b) In a number, the ten thousands place is 1, the thousands place is 2 and the hundreds place is 3. The number is (   ).

     A. 123   B. 1230   C. 12 300

   (c) In a four-digit number, the sum of all the digits is 36. The number is (   ).

     A. 3600   B. 9999   C. 6666

   (d) In a four-digit number, the product of all the digits is 1. The number is (   ).

     A. 1000   B. 1100   C. 1111

Challenge and extension questions

⑥ In a four-digit number, the sum of all the four digits is 2. Write all such numbers.

⑦ Give some real-life examples in which numbers more than 1000 are used.

2.2   Knowing numbers beyond 1000 (2)

Learning objective

Compare and order four-digit numbers

Basic questions

1 Count in multiples of a number and fill in the blanks.

(a) 1, 2, 3, ____ , ____ , ____ , 7, ____ , ____ , ____ .

(b) 10, 20, 30, ____ , ____ , ____ , 70, ____ , ____ , ____ .

(c) 100, 200, 300, ____ , ____ , ____ , 700, ____ , ____ , ____ .

(d) 1000, 2000, 3000, ____ , ____ , ____ , 7000, ____ , ____ , ____ .

(e) 0, 25, 50, 75, ____ , ____ , ____ , 175, ____ , ____ , ____ .

2 Write all the numbers based on the given information.

(a) Numbers that come before and after each number.

(   ), 1738, (   )   (   ), 9999, (   )

(   ), 4106, (   )   (   ), 6000, (   )

(b) Whole tens that come before and after each number.

(   ), 3900, (   )   (   ), 1550, (   )

(   ), 7809, (   )   (   ), 6000, (   )

(c) Whole hundreds that come before and after each number.

(   ), 2657, (   )   (   ), 4505, (   )

(   ), 7790, (   )   (   ), 6000, (   )

(d) Whole thousands that come before and after each number.

(   ), 1067, (   )   (   ), 9222, (   )

(   ), 4050, (   )   (   ), 6000, (   )

3 Count and complete the number patterns.

(a) 234, 235, 236, (   ), (   ).

(b) 1000, 1025, 1050, (   ), (   ), 1125.

(c) 500, 2500, 4500, (   ), (   ).

(d) 9000, 8000, 7000, (   ), (   ), 4000.

(e) 3500, 3000, 2500, (   ), (   ), (   ), (   ), (   ).

4 Fill in the blanks with the following numbers.

10, 920, 6000, 5010, 1000, 3280, 8880, 6540, 4990.

(a) The numbers greater than 3000 but less than 6000 are _____

_____ .

(b) The number that is 5000 more than 1000 is _____ .

(c) The whole thousands are _____ .

(d) Put all the above four-digit numbers in order starting from the greatest: _____ .

Challenge and extension questions

5 Choose four of the five digits 2, 3, 6, 8 and 0 to form four-digit numbers. What is the least possible number? (   ). How about the greatest possible number? (   ).

6 When you write numbers from 7000 to 8000, you need to write 7 (   ) times, 8 (   ) times and 9 (   ) times.

2.3 Rounding numbers to the nearest 10, 100 and 1000

 Learning objective

Round numbers to the nearest 10, 100 and 1000

 Basic questions

1 Write the number that each letter stands for.

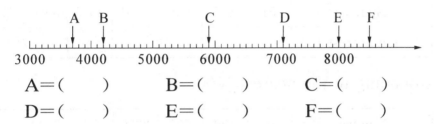

A = ( )   B = ( )   C = ( )

D = ( )   E = ( )   F = ( )

2 Mark the numbers on the number line.

```
|‥‥|‥‥|‥‥|‥‥|‥‥|‥‥|‥‥|‥‥|‥‥|‥‥|→
0   1000 2000 3000 4000 5000 6000 7000 8000 9000 10 000
```

A = 500   B = 6000   C = 8100   D = 1600   E = 3500   F = 9900

3 In question 2, all the numbers A, B, C, D, E and F are between 0 and 10 000. Compare the distances of each number to these two numbers on the number line, and fill in the brackets.

(a) The numbers that are nearer to 0 are (   ).

(b) The numbers that are nearer to 10 000 are (   ).

4 True or false. (Put a √ for true and a × for false; you may use number lines to help yourself.)

(a) Rounding 19 to its nearest 10, the result is 20.   (   )

(b) Rounding 19 to its nearest 100, the result is 200.   (   )

(c) Rounding 19 to its nearest 1000, the result is 2000.   (   )

(d) Rounding 5890 to its nearest 1000, the result is 6000. (   )

(e) Rounding 8850 to its nearest 1000, the result is 9000. (　)

(f) Rounding 9549 to its nearest 1000, the result is 10 000.　(　)

5 Round the numbers to their nearest numbers as indicated.

(a) Rounding to the nearest 10.

Number	35	9	91	501	199	2021	4093	9999
To the nearest 10								

(b) Rounding to the nearest 100.

Number	51	325	956	1501	3020	5050	8116	9999
To the nearest 100								

(c) Rounding to the nearest 1000.

Number	20	199	501	2300	4708	7499	8499	9999
To the nearest 1000								

Challenge and extension questions

6 I am a number. When I am rounded to the nearest 10, the result is 50. When I am rounded to the nearest 100, the result is 0. Please find all the numbers that I can possibly be.

7 I am a number. When I am rounded to the nearest 10, the result is 7000. When I am rounded to the nearest 100, the result is 7000. When I am rounded to the nearest 1000, the result is still 7000. I am not 7000. Please find all the numbers that I can possibly be.

2.4　Addition with four-digit numbers (1)

Learning objective

Add numbers with up to 4 digits

Basic questions

1 Calculate with reasoning.

(a) Kim's method.

$3130 + 4216 = $ ___

> Thousands＋Thousands：$3000＋4000=$ _____
> Hundreds＋Hundreds：$100＋200=$ ___
> Tens＋Tens：$30＋10=$ ___
> Ones＋Ones：$0＋6=$ ___
> ___ ＋ ___ ＋ ___ ＋ ___ ＝ ___

$2068 + 1107 = $ ___

> Thousands＋Thousands：___ ＋ ___ ＝ ___
> Hundreds＋Hundreds：___ ＋ ___ ＝ ___
> Tens＋Tens：___ ＋ ___ ＝ ___
> Ones＋Ones：___ ＋ ___ ＝ ___
> ___ ＋ ___ ＋ ___ ＋ ___ ＝ ___

(b) Andy's method.

$7132 + 1454 = $ ___

> Ones＋Ones：___ ＋ ___ ＝ ___
> Tens＋Tens：___ ＋ ___ ＝ ___
> Hundreds＋Hundreds：___ ＋ ___ ＝ ___
> Thousands＋Thousands：___ ＋ ___ ＝ ___
> ___ ＋ ___ ＋ ___ ＋ ___ ＝ ___

$$3063 + 4705 = \_\_\_\_$$

Ones＋Ones: ___ ＋ ___ ＝ ___	
Tens＋Tens: ___ ＋ ___ ＝ ___	
Hundreds＋Hundreds: ___ ＋ ___ ＝ ___	
Thousands＋Thousands: ___ ＋ ___ ＝ ___	
____ ＋ ____ ＋ ____ ＋ ____ ＝ ____	

(c) Joe's method.

$$3024 + 2509$$
$$= 3024 + 2000 + 500 + 9$$
$$= \_\_\_ + \_\_\_ + \_\_\_$$
$$= \_\_\_ + \_\_\_$$
$$= \_\_\_$$

$$3175 + 1423$$
$$= 3175 + \_\_\_ + \_\_\_ + \_\_\_ + \_\_\_$$
$$= \_\_\_ + \_\_\_ + \_\_\_$$
$$= \_\_\_ + \_\_\_$$
$$= \_\_\_$$

(d) Emma's method.

$$4130 + 3512$$
$$= 4130 + 2 + 10 + 500 + 3000$$
$$= \_\_\_ + \_\_\_ + \_\_\_ + \_\_\_$$
$$= \_\_\_ + \_\_\_ + \_\_\_$$
$$= \_\_\_ + \_\_\_$$
$$= \_\_\_$$

$$1782 + 7219$$
$$= 1782 + \_\_\_ + \_\_\_ + \_\_\_ + \_\_\_$$
$$= \_\_\_ + \_\_\_ + \_\_\_ + \_\_\_$$
$$= \_\_\_ + \_\_\_ + \_\_\_$$
$$= \_\_\_ + \_\_\_$$
$$= \_\_\_$$

2 Use your preferred method to calculate. Show your working.

5136＋8121   4228＋2436   6750＋3128

3 First use the 6 number cards below to form 3 addition sentences of adding 2 four-digit numbers. Then work them out with your preferred method.

| 6 | 8 | 9 | 3 | 5 | 0 |

(a) _____   (b) _____   (c) _____

4 Write the number sentences and calculate.

(a) What number is 1000 more than 1554?

(b) What number is 1000 less than 5528?

(c) One addend is 2139 and the other addend is 3324. What is the sum?

Challenge and extension question

5 Fill in the brackets.

(a) The sum of the least four-digit number and the least three-digit number is a (   )-digit number.

(b) The sum of the greatest four-digit number and the least three-digit number is a (   )-digit number.

(c) The sum of two four-digit numbers can be a (   )-digit number or a (   )-digit number.

2.5 Addition with four-digit numbers (2)

 Learning objective

Add numbers with up to 4 digits

 Basic questions

1. Use the column method to calculate.

    (a) 3500+1234=

    3 5 0 0
    + 1 2 3 4
    ‾‾‾‾‾‾‾

    (b) 308+7123=

        3 0 8
    + 7 1 2 3
    ‾‾‾‾‾‾‾

    (c) 7095+225=

        7 0 9 5
    +   2 2 5
    ‾‾‾‾‾‾‾

    (d) 5907+180=

    (e) 5372+1043+2301=

2. Fill in the table.

Addend	1327	3204	584	1178	1257	9178
Addend	1150	2328	4265	7433	4465	822
Sum						

3. Is each of the following correct? Put a √ if it is and a × otherwise and make the correction.

    (a)
       3 8 0 1
    +   2 0 3
    ‾‾‾‾‾‾‾
      5 8 3 1
      (   )

    (b)
      7 0 9 1
    + 2 0 6 1
    ‾‾‾‾‾‾‾
      9 0 5 2
      (   )

    (c)
         5 2 4
    +   9 8 2
    ‾‾‾‾‾‾‾
    1 4 1 0 6
      (   )

4 Give this a try.

(a) 32 145+25 134=

```
    3  2  1  4  5
+   2  5  1  3  4
_____
```

(b) 7408+6925=

```
    7  4  0  8
+   6  9  2  5
_____
```

5 Application problems.

(a) Andrew walked 1200 metres in the morning and 1300 metres in the afternoon. How far did he walk that day?

(b) Sara earned £2580 in July and £2880 in August. How much did she earn in the two months?

(c) A factory consumed 3326 kilowatts of electricity in the winter season in a year and 2539 kilowatts in the spring season. What is the total usage of the electricity in these two seasons?

Challenge and extension question

6 Fill in the ☐ with suitable numbers.

```
  ☐  9  ☐  ☐
+ 3  ☐  3  3
_____
  7  7  5  5
```

```
    ☐  6
+ ☐ ☐  2  ☐
_____
  2  7  1  8
```

```
  5  3  7  ☐
+ ☐ ☐ ☐  ☐  2
_____
  3  3  3  0  0
```

2.6 Subtractions with four-digit numbers (1)

Learning objective

Subtract numbers with up to 4 digits

Basic questions

1 Calculate with reasoning.

(a) Donald's method.

$5487 - 3245 = $ ____

| Thousands—Thousands: $5000 - 3000 = $ ____ |
| Hundreds—Hundreds: $400 - 200 = $ ____ |
| Tens—Tens: $80 - 40 = $ ____ |
| Ones—Ones: $7 - 5 = $ ____ |
| ____ $+$ ____ $+$ ____ $+$ ____ $= $ ____ |

$9746 - 5443 = $ ____

| Subtract thousands first: $9746 - 5000 = $ ____ |
| Then subtract hundreds: ____ $-$ ____ $= $ ____ |
| Then subtract tens: ____ $-$ ____ $= $ |
| Finally subtract ones: ____ $-$ ____ $= $ ____ |

(b) Amy's method.

$7965 - 5342 = $ ____

| Thousands—Thousands: ____ $-$ ____ $= $ ____ |
| Hundreds—Hundreds: ____ $-$ ____ $= $ ____ |
| Tens—Tens: ____ $-$ ____ $= $ ____ |
| Ones—Ones: ____ $-$ ____ $= $ ____ |
| ____ $+$ ____ $+$ ____ $+$ ____ $= $ ____ |

6957－3356＝＿＿＿＿

| Subtract thousands first: ＿＿＿ － ＿＿＿ ＝ ＿＿＿ |
| Then subtract hundreds: ＿＿＿ － ＿＿＿ ＝ ＿＿＿ |
| Then subtract tens: ＿＿＿ － ＿＿＿ ＝ ＿＿＿ |
| Finally subtract ones: ＿＿＿ － ＿＿＿ ＝ ＿＿＿ |

(c) Joe's method.

$5306－2285$
$＝5306－2000－200－80－5$
$＝\underline{\quad}－\underline{\quad}－\underline{\quad}－\underline{\quad}$
$＝\underline{\quad}－\underline{\quad}－\underline{\quad}$
$＝\underline{\quad}－\underline{\quad}$
$＝\underline{\quad}$

$6238－1729$
$＝6238－\underline{\quad}－\underline{\quad}－\underline{\quad}－\underline{\quad}$
$＝\underline{\quad}－\underline{\quad}－\underline{\quad}－\underline{\quad}$
$＝\underline{\quad}－\underline{\quad}－\underline{\quad}$
$＝\underline{\quad}－\underline{\quad}$
$＝\underline{\quad}$

(d) Emma's method.

$9008－3627$
$＝9008－7－20－600－3000$
$＝\underline{\quad}－\underline{\quad}－\underline{\quad}－\underline{\quad}$
$＝\underline{\quad}－\underline{\quad}－\underline{\quad}$
$＝\underline{\quad}－\underline{\quad}$
$＝\underline{\quad}$

$8536－3097$
$＝8536－\underline{\quad}－\underline{\quad}－\underline{\quad}$
$＝\underline{\quad}－\underline{\quad}－\underline{\quad}－\underline{\quad}$
$＝\underline{\quad}－\underline{\quad}－\underline{\quad}$
$＝\underline{\quad}－\underline{\quad}$
$＝\underline{\quad}$

2 Use your preferred method to calculate. Show your working.

(a) 7759－4325 (b) 5000－2169 (c) 8439－7346

(d) 9557－6262 (e) 4821－2656 (f) 6668－1095

③ Use the six number cards below to form subtraction sentences that subtract a four-digit number from another four-digit number. Then use your preferred method to calculate.

| 9 | 3 | 2 | 8 | 5 | 0 |

(a) _____   (b) _____   (c) _____

④ Write the number sentences and calculate.

(a) A number is 3415 less than 5032. What is the number?

(b) The minuend is 9418 and the subtrahend is 2280. What is the difference?

Challenge and extension question

⑤ The mass of one box of apples and one box of pears is 7450 grams. The mass of two boxes of apples and one box of pears is 9550 grams. Write the number sentences and calculate:

(a) What is the mass of one box of apples?

(b) What is the mass of one box of pears?

2.7 Subtraction with four-digit numbers (2)

Learning objective

Subtract numbers with up to 4 digits

Basic questions

1 Use the column method to calculate.

(a) $5685 - 2453 =$

```
  5 6 8 5
- 2 4 5 3
─────────
```

(b) $3149 - 778 =$

```
  3 1 4 9
-   7 7 8
─────────
```

(c) $5151 - 4279 =$

```
  5 1 5 1
- 4 2 7 9
─────────
```

(d) $7435 - 3267 =$ (e) $5507 - 3368 =$ (f) $1001 - 703 + 5689 =$

2 Is each of the following correct? Put a $\checkmark$ if it is and a $\times$ otherwise and make the correction.

(a)
```
  3 4 5 5
- 1 1 0 9
─────────
  2 3 5 6
  (   )
```

(b)
```
  6 5 1 7
- 3 2 2 6
─────────
  3 3 3 1
  (   )
```

(c)
```
  8 0 0 5
- 7 3 9 6
─────────
  1 6 1 9
  (   )
```

3 Fill in the table.

Minuend	8738	9564	4657	6771	5316	7008
Subtrahend	1534	5268	2476	6635	2138	6569
Difference						

4 Fill in the ☐ with suitable numbers.

(a)
```
  ☐ 5 ☐ ☐
−   4 ☐ 5 9
─────────────
    3 5 3 8
```

(b)
```
  ☐ 4 0 ☐
−   7 ☐ ☐ 5
─────────────
    1 2 0 5
```

(c)
```
    6 7 ☐ 3
−     ☐ 3 ☐
─────────────
    6 3 4 8
```

5 Give this a try.

(a) 65 077−43 015＝

```
    6 5 0 7 7
−   4 3 0 1 5
─────────────
```

(b) 11 078−8569＝

```
    1 1 0 7 8
−     8 5 6 9
─────────────
```

6 The flight distances from London to Amsterdam, Beijing and New York are 358 km, 8161 km and 5586 km, respectively.

(a) What is the difference between the distance from London to Amsterdam and that from London to Beijing?

(b) On a business trip, Joe flew from New York to London on the first day and then from London to Beijing on the second day. Which day did he fly longer and by how much? What was the total flight distance he flew in the two days?

 Challenge and extension question

7 What number does ☐ stand for in each case below?

```
    8 ☐ 6 2
−   7 9 5 5
─────────────
```

(a) If the difference is a four-digit number, the number in the ☐ must be (   ).

(b) If the difference is a three-digit number, the greatest possible number in the ☐ is (   ).

2.8 Estimating and checking answers using inverse operations

Learning objective

Estimate and check answers to a calculation

Basic questions

1 Work out the answers mentally. What do you find?

$5200 + 800 =$	$3100 - 900 =$	$6700 + 2000 =$	$9020 - 220 =$
$6000 - 800 =$	$3100 - 2200 =$	$8700 - 2000 =$	$9020 - 8800 =$
$6000 - 5200 =$	$2200 + 900 =$	$8700 - 6700 =$	$8800 + 220 =$

2 Round the following numbers to the nearest 10 100 and 1000.

	2132	5522	4590	6705	1848	8999
Nearest 10						
Nearest 100						
Nearest 1000						

3 Estimate to the nearest 100 and then calculate.

$2012 + 1689$	$5431 + 3309$	$5996 + 2992 + 889$
Estimate:_____	Estimate:_____	Estimate:_____
Calculate: _____	Calculate: _____	Calculate: _____

$5674 - 2318$	$7883 - 5479 - 2078$	$9989 - 2994 + 3030$
Estimate:_____	Estimate:_____	Estimate:_____
Calculate:_____	Calculate:_____	Calculate:_____

4 Estimate to the nearest 1000 first and then calculate.

$1308 + 4117$	$3657 + 6329$	$5291 + 1428 + 3049$
Estimate: _____	Estimate: _____	Estimate: _____
Calculate: _____	Calculate: _____	Calculate: _____

$9417 - 7206$	$6529 - 780 - 2115$	$7658 - 2300 + 3100$
Estimate: _____	Estimate: _____	Estimate: _____
Calculate: _____	Calculate: _____	Calculate: _____

5 Use the column method to calculate and then use inverse operations to check your answers. If an answer is wrong, then correct it. (Note: addition and subtraction are inverse operations to each other. The first one has been done for you.)

(a)
```
  3 4 0 5
+ 1 5 3 5
---------
  4 9 4 0
```
Check: Does $4940 - 1535 = 3405$?
Yes, it checks.

(b)
```
  5 5 4 8
+ 4 3 7 1
---------
  9 8 1 9
```
Check:

(c)
```
  9 2 0 8
- 3 2 5 7
---------
  5 0 5 1
```
Check:

(d)
```
  8 3 9 9
+   6 9 9
---------
  8 9 8 8
```
Check:

(e)
```
  4 0 3 2
- 2 3 9 1
---------
  1 6 4 1
```
Check:

(f)
```
 1 0 0 0 0
-    4 0 7 5
-----------
   5 0 2 5
```
Check:

6 Application problems.

(a) A farmer has two water tanks. The larger one has a capacity of 5230 litres and the smaller one has a capacity of 1755 litres. What is the difference between the capacities of the water tanks? What is their total capacity?

(b) A company plans to spend £5850 on office computers and £1750 on printers.

  (i) If the budget for the two items is £7000, estimate whether the budget is sufficient for purchasing the two items.

  (ii) If the budget is not sufficient, how much more money is needed to purchase the two items?

 Challenge and extension question

7 A number consists of four digits 8, 8, 6 and 2.

  (a) Adding the number and 2500, the result is between 5000 and 6000. This number is (   ).

  (b) Subtracting 2500 from the number, the result is between 3500 and 4000. This number is (   ).

Unit test 2

1 Work these out mentally, then write the answers.

$3000 + 2000 =$ $8690 - 690 =$ $5240 + 4750 =$

$2500 + 4500 =$ $7190 - 4190 =$ $6070 - 3010 =$

$9540 - 9450 =$ $7000 + ($ $) = 10\,000$ $($ $) - 3220 = 5000$

2 Write the numbers that each letter stands for.

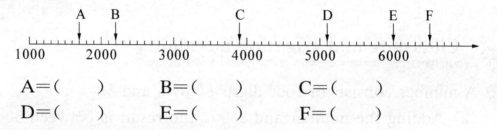

A=(   )   B=(   )   C=(   )

D=(   )   E=(   )   F=(   )

3 Count and complete the number patterns.

(a) 505, 510, 515, (   ), (   ), 530.

(b) 505, 605, 705, (   ), (   ), 1005.

(c) 5000, 6000, 7000, (   ), (   ), 10 000.

(d) 200, 175, 150, (   ), (   ).

(e) 12, 24, 36, (   ), (   ), (   ), 84.

4 Complete the place value chart.

3019

Thousands	Hundreds	Tens	Ones

7909

Thousands	Hundreds	Tens	Ones

1535

Thousands	Hundreds	Tens	Ones

1000

Ten thousands	Thousands	Hundreds	Tens	Ones

5 Use the column method to calculate. (Check the answers to the questions marked with * .)

(a) * $5939+811=$ (b) * $10\,000-8917$ (c) * $3892+4308=$

(d) $8917-7289+1023=$ (e) $5003+2085-3999=$

6 Estimate to the nearest 1000 first. Then calculate.

$3771+2117$ $1181+8807-3500$

Estimate:_____   Estimate:_____

Calculate: _____   Calculate:_____

$8512-3296$ $9389-7209+2311$

Estimate:_____   Estimate:_____

Calculate: _____   Calculate: _____

7 Write the number sentences and then find the answers.

(a) What number is 1000 less than 10 000?

(b) The sum of two addends is 8569. One addend is 3378. What is the other addend?

(c) The subtrahend is 8288 and the difference is 3009. What is the minuend?

8 A shop earned £8050 in July and £9558 in August by selling local and seasonal foods.

(a) How much did the shop earn in these two months?

(b) How much more did it earn in August than in July?

9 There are 1337 pupils in Year 7, 1021 pupils in Year 8 and 1368 pupils in Year 9. How many pupils are there in total in these three grades?

10 The flight distance from London to Rome is 1434 km and that from London to Oslo is 1157 km. Jane plans to fly from Rome to London on the first day and then from London to Oslo on the second day.

(a) On which day will Jane fly longer, and by how much?

(b) What is the total flight distance Jan will travel in these two days?

Chapter 3   Multiplying by a two-digit number

3.1   Multiplying whole tens by a two-digit number

 Learning objective

Multiply numbers by multiples of ten

 Basic questions

1 Calculate with reasoning.

(a)
4	
40	×12=
400	

(b)
450	
45	×7=
4500	

Fill in the blanks.

(c) $40×12=10×4×12=10×\underline{\hspace{1.5cm}}=\underline{\hspace{1.5cm}}$

(d) $450×7=10×45×7=10×\underline{\hspace{1.5cm}}=\underline{\hspace{1.5cm}}$

(e) $400×12=100×4×12=100×\underline{\hspace{1.5cm}}=\underline{\hspace{1.5cm}}$

(f) $4500×7=100×45×7=100×\underline{\hspace{1.5cm}}=\underline{\hspace{1.5cm}}$

2 Observe carefully and write the answers.

$11×2=$	$3×15=$	$45×6=$
$110×2=$	$30×15=$	$450×6=$
$11×200=$	$3×1500=$	$450×60=$
$110×20=$	$300×15=$	$4500×6=$

3 Complete the following mental sums.

$63×60=$	$100×30=$	$4×250=$	$17×20=$
$42×30=$	$50×18=$	$75×30=$	$160×9=$
$6×1500=$	$2×50=$	$88×30=$	$700×17=$
$13×500=$	$8×400=$	$6×110=$	$5400×6=$

4 Fill in ◯ with >, <or＝without calculation.

250×40 ◯ 40×250 1300×4 ◯ 13×40

6500×330 ◯ 650×330 47×210 ◯ 470×210

5 Think carefully and calculate the following.

(a) $34 \times 6 = ($ $)$

$30 \times 6 = ($ $)$

$4 \times 6 = ($ $)$

$(30 \times 6) + (4 \times 6) = ($ $)$

When you work on a number sentence with brackets, perform calculations inside the brackets first.

(b) $52 \times 7 = ($ $)$

$50 \times 7 = ($ $)$

$2 \times 7 = ($ $)$

$(50 \times 7) + (2 \times 7) = ($ $)$

6 True or false.

(a) $50 \times 21 = 50 \times (20+1) = 50 \times 20 + 1 = 1000 + 1 = 1001$

(   )

(b) $50 \times 21 = 50 \times (20+1) = 50 \times 20 + 50 \times 1 = 1000 + 50 = 1050$

(   )

(c) $29 \times 30 = (30-1) \times 30 = 30 \times 30 - 1 \times 30 = 900 - 30 = 870$

(   )

(d) Given three numbers A, B and C, we have

$A \times (B+C) = A \times B + A \times C$ (   )

$A \times (B-C) = A \times B - A \times C$ (   )

7 Calculate smartly. The first one has been done for you.

(a) $35 \times 7 + 35 \times 3$

$= 35 \times (7 + 3)$

$= 35 \times 10$

$= 350$

(b) $159 \times 32 - 59 \times 32$

$= (159 - 59) \times 32$

$=$

$=$

(c) $656 \times 62 - 56 \times 62$

(d) $62 \times 98 + 38 \times 98$

8 Write the number sentences and then calculate.

(a) What is 12 times 60?

(b) What is the sum of 800 twenty-fives?

9

50p/bottle

70p/bottle

There are 24 bottles in each pack. How much do they cost in total? (Please use two different methods to answer.)

Method 1:   Method 2:

Challenge and extension question

10 In each number sentence below, fill in the two boxes with the same two-digit number so the equation is true. The first one has been done for you.

(a) $5 \times \boxed{50} = 2 \boxed{50}$

(b) $6 \times \boxed{} = 3 \boxed{}$

(c) $9 \times \boxed{} = 4 \boxed{}$

3.2 Multiplying a two-digit number by a two-digit number (1)

 Learning objective

Use different methods to multiply two-digit numbers together

Basic questions

① Work these out mentally, and then write the answers.

(a) $16 \times 10 =$

(b) $16 \times 5 =$

(c) $16 \times 10 + 16 \times 5 =$

> When you work on a number sentence like this, perform all the multiplications/divisions first and then perform the additions/subtractions.

(d) $16 \times 10 + 16 \times 15 = 16 \times \boxed{}$

(e) $24 \times 10 =$

(f) $24 \times 5 =$

(g) $24 \times 10 + 24 \times 5 =$

(h) $24 \times 10 + 24 \times 5 = 24 \times \boxed{}$

(i) $33 \times 10 =$

(j) $33 \times 5 =$

(k) $33 \times 10 + 33 \times 5 =$

(l) $33 \times 10 + 33 \times 5 = 33 \times \boxed{}$

② Estimate first and then calculate.

(a) What is 13 twenty-fours?

Estimate: The answer is between (   ) and (   ).

Calculate: $13 \times 20 = \boxed{}$

$13 \times 4 = \boxed{}$

$13 \times 24 = \boxed{}$

(b) What is 31 sixty-twos?

Estimate: The answer is between (   ) and (   ).

Calculate: $31 \times 60 = \boxed{}$

$31 \times 2 = \boxed{}$

$31 \times 62 = \boxed{}$

③ Calculate with different methods.

48×25

$= \boxed{12} \times \boxed{4} \times \boxed{}$

$=$

$=$

48×25

$= \boxed{40} \times \boxed{} + \boxed{8} \times \boxed{}$

$=$

$=$

48×25

$= \boxed{50} \times \boxed{} - \boxed{2} \times \boxed{}$

$=$

$=$

Do you have other methods to calculate?

④ Calculate.

19×21

$= 19 \times 20 + 19 \times \boxed{}$

$=$

$=$

33×77

$= 33 \times \boxed{} + 33 \times \boxed{}$

$=$

$=$

51×63

$=$

$=$

$=$

⑤ Write the number sentences and then calculate.

(a) What is the product of 11 times 55?

(b) How much more is 550 than 19 times 19?

Challenge and extension question

⑥ In the calculation below, each letter represents one number. Different letters represent different numbers. What numbers do they represent in order to make the calculation correct?

$$
\begin{array}{r}
1\ A\ B\ C\ D\ E \\
\times \qquad\qquad 3 \\
\hline
A\ B\ C\ D\ E\ 1
\end{array}
$$

A=_____   B=_____   C=_____   D=_____   E=_____

3.3 Multiplying a two-digit number by a two-digit number (2)

 Learning objective

Use formal written methods to multiply two-digit numbers together

 Basic questions

1 Work these out mentally, then write the answers.

$180 + 135 =$ $53 \times 7 =$ $640 - 480 =$ $15 \times 2 \times 5 =$

$580 + 472 =$ $70 \div 70 + 2 =$ $60 \times 700 =$ $95 \div 5 =$

$220 \times 4 =$ $25 \times 80 =$ $12 \times 55 =$ $3000 \div 4 =$

2 Fill in the boxes to complete the column calculation.

$48 \times 65 =$ ☐

```
        4  8
×       6  5
─────────────
   ☐  ☐  ☐     ----► First multiply 48 and ☐ in the ones place.
   ☐  ☐  ☐     ----► Then multiply 48 and ☐ in the tens place.
─────────────
 ☐  ☐  ☐  ☐
```

3 Try it on your own and use the column method to calculate the following.

$13 \times 22 =$ $75 \times 99 =$ $63 \times 48 =$

4 Where are the mistakes? Please identify them first and then correct them.

(a) $44 \times 55 = 440$

```
      4 4
  ×   5 5
  ─────────
    2 2 0
    2 2 0
  ─────────
    4 4 0
```

(b) $37 \times 12 = 111$

```
      3 7
  ×   1 2
  ─────────
      7 4
      3 7
  ─────────
    1 1 1
```

(c) $26 \times 98 = 442$

```
      2 6
  ×   9 8
  ─────────
    2 0 8
    2 3 4
  ─────────
    4 4 2
```

My correction:

5 Write the number sentences and then calculate.

(a) What is the product of two eighty-nines?

(b) What is the product of the two greatest two-digit numbers?

6 Application problems.

(a) In a fundraising campaign for flood victims, Year 1 pupils donated £99 and the amount their teachers donated was 33 times as much. How much did the pupils and teachers donate altogether?

(b) In a tree-planting activity organised by a school, 53 participating pupils were from Year 3. The number of pupils from Year 4 was the same. The number of pupils who took part from Year 5 was twice the total number of the pupils from Year 3 and Year 4. How many pupils in Year 5 took part in the tree-planting activity?

Challenge and extension question

7 Calculate and try to remember the answers.　Find the patterns.

$11 \times 11 =$	$11 \times 11 =$
$12 \times 12 =$	$12 \times 11 =$
$13 \times 13 =$	$13 \times 11 =$
$14 \times 14 =$	$14 \times 11 =$
$15 \times 15 =$	$15 \times 11 =$
$16 \times 16 =$	$16 \times 11 =$
$17 \times 17 =$	$17 \times 11 =$
$18 \times 18 =$	$18 \times 11 =$
$19 \times 19 =$	$19 \times 11 =$

3.4 Multiplying a three-digit number by a two-digit number (1)

 Learning objective

Use different methods to multiply three-digit numbers by two-digit numbers

 Basic questions

1. Work these out mentally, and then write the answers.

   $125 \times 3 =$ $125 \times 5 =$ $125 \times 7 =$ $125 + 375 =$

   $125 + 200 =$ $125 + 500 =$ $125 + 625 =$ $125 \times 9 =$

   $125 \times 4 =$ $125 \times 6 =$ $125 \times 8 =$ $125 \times 11 =$

2. Estimate first and then calculate.

   (a) What is 112 forty-sixes?

   Estimate: The answer is between (　　) and (　　).

   Calculate: $112 \times 40 = \boxed{}$

   $112 \times 6 = \boxed{}$

   $112 \times 46 = \boxed{}$

   (b) What is 229 twenty-ones?

   Estimate: The answer is between (　　) and (　　).

   Calculate: $229 \times 20 = \boxed{}$

   $229 \times 1 = \boxed{}$

   $229 \times 21 = \boxed{}$

3 Fill in the boxes to complete the column calculation.

$418 \times 65 = \boxed{}$

```
        4   1   8
×           6   5
─────────────────────
    □   □   □   □    ----→ First multiply 418 by 5 in the ones place.
    □   □   □        ----→ Then multiply 418 by 6 in the tens place.
─────────────────────
  □   □   □   □   □
```

4 Fill in the boxes with suitable numbers.

```
      1   2   3
×         4   5
───────────────
      6   1   5  ······123×□
  4   9   2      ······123×□
───────────────
  5   5   3   5
```

```
      3   5   7
×         8   9
───────────────
  3   2   1   3  ······□×□
  2   8   5   6  ······□×□
───────────────
  3   1   7   7   3
```

5 Use the column method to calculate.

$327 \times 11 =$ $256 \times 32 =$ $555 \times 99 =$

6 Write the number sentences and then calculate.

(a) What is the sum of 222 fifty-fives?

(b) What is the product of the greatest two-digit number multiplied by the greatest three-digit number?

7 Application problem.

£329

£300 less than 12 times
the price of the microwave

How much do the two items cost in total?

Challenge and extension question

8 (a) It took Alvin 100 seconds to walk from the first floor to the fifth floor. How many seconds will it take him to walk to the eleventh floor if he continues at the same pace?

(b) A convoy of 52 trucks stopped for inspection. Each truck was 4 metres long. The distance between two trucks was 6 metres. The total length of the convoy was (   ) metres.

3.5 Multiplying a three-digit number by a two-digit number (2)

 Learning objective

Use formal written methods to multiply three-digit numbers by two-digit numbers

 Basic questions

1 Work these out mentally, and then write the answers.

$14 \times 2 =$	$6 \times 5 =$	$13 \times 3 =$
$140 \times 2 =$	$60 \times 5 =$	$13 \times 30 =$
$140 \times 20 =$	$60 \times 500 =$	$130 \times 300 =$

2 Give it a try.

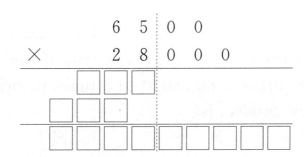

3 Write a suitable number in each box. The first one has been done for you.

(a) 28×500

$= 28 \times 5 \times \boxed{100}$

$= \boxed{140} \times \boxed{100}$

$= \boxed{14\,000}$

(b) 220×400

$= 220 \times 4 \times \boxed{}$

$= \boxed{} \times \boxed{}$

$= \boxed{}$

(c) 560×120

$= 560 \times 12 \times \boxed{}$

$= \boxed{} \times \boxed{}$

$= \boxed{}$

4 Fill in the box based on $32 \times 45 = 1440$. The first one has been done for you.

(a) $320 \times \boxed{4500} = 1\,440\,000$ (b) $32 \times \boxed{} = 1\,440\,000$

(c) $\boxed{} \times 450 = 1\,440\,000$ (d) $\boxed{} \times 45 = 1\,440\,000$

5 Multiple choice questions. (Note: when two numbers are multiplied, the result is called the product, and the two numbers are called the factors, so product=factor×factor.)

(a) In calculating 246×75, the product of multiplying 246 by the digit 7 in the tens place of the factor 75 is (   ).

A. 17 220   B. 1722   C. 1 722 000   D. 172 200

(b) When 225 is added for 15 times, the sum is (   ). (Hint: count $225 + 225$ as 225 being added twice.)

A. 33 750   B. 337 500   C. 3 375 000   D. 3375

(c) When one factor has 2 zeros at the end and the other factor has 1 zero at the end, then the product has (   ) zeros at the end.

A. 2   B. 3   C. at least 3   D. 4

(d) The product of two factors is 120. If one factor is doubled and the other is increased to 5 times its original value, then the new product is(   ).

A. 1200   B. 360   C. 900   D. 180

6 Use the column method to calculate.

(a) $349 \times 57 =$ (b) $608 \times 22 =$ (c) $4200 \times 150 =$

(d) $39 \times 208 =$ (e) $26 \times 737 =$ (f) $404 \times 88 =$

7 Write the number sentences and then calculate.

(a) A is 200, B is 12 times as large as A and C is 12 times as large as B. What is C?

(b) The divisor is 160. Both the quotient and the remainder are 50. What is the dividend?

 Challenge and extension question

8 There are 20 classes in a school and each class has 32 pupils. A cinema has 1000 seats. Is this enough to seat all the pupils? If so, how many seats will be left available?

3.6 Dividing two-digit or three-digit numbers by tens

Learning objective

Use different methods to divide three-digit numbers by multiples of ten

Basic questions

1 Work these out mentally, then write the answers.

$80 \div 2 =$ $150 \div 5 =$ $840 \div 7 =$ $630 \div 9 =$

$80 \div 20 =$ $150 \div 50 =$ $840 \div 70 =$ $630 \div 90 =$

2 What is the greatest number you can fill in each pair of brackets below?

$50 \times ($ $) < 157$ $($ $) \times 30 < 231$ $70 \times ($ $) < 369$

$($ $) \times 40 < 369$ $80 \times ($ $) < 508$ $($ $) \times 90 < 396$

3 Think carefully and then fill in the brackets. The first one has been done for you.

(a) $92 \div 40 = ?$

Think: In $9 \div 4$, the quotient is (2).

In $92 \div 40$, the quotient is (2).

$92 - 40 \times (2) = (12)$.

$92 \div 40 = (2)$ r (12).

(b) $362 \div 40 = ?$

Think: In $36 \div 4$, the quotient is (   ).

In $362 \div 40$, the quotient is (   ).

$362 - 40 \times ($ $) = ($ $)$.

$362 \div 40 = ($ $)$ r $($ $)$.

(c) $75 \div 20 = ?$

Think: How many 20s are there in 75?

$20 \times ($ $) < 75,$

$20 \times ($ $) > 75,$

There are (   ) 20s in 75.

Then: in $75 \div 20$, the quotient is (   ).

So: $75 \div 20 = ($ $)$ r (   ).

(d) $256 \div 30 = ?$

Think: How many 30s are there in 256?

$30 \times ($ $) < 256,$

$30 \times ($ $) > 256,$

There are (   ) 30s in 256.

Then: in $256 \div 30$, the quotient is (   ).

So: $256 \div 30 = ($ $)$ r (   ).

4 Use the column method to calculate. The first one has been done for you.

(a) $96 \div 60 = 1$ r 36 (b) $145 \div 20 =$ (c) $572 \div 80 =$

$$
\begin{array}{r}
1 \\
60\overline{)\,9\ \ 6} \\
6\ \ 0 \\
\hline
3\ \ 6
\end{array}
$$

(d) $360 \div 70 =$ (e) $455 \div 50 =$ (f) $666 \div 90 =$

5 Write the number sentences and then calculate.

(a) 292 is divided by 60. What is the quotient? What is the remainder?

(b) What are the quotient and remainder of the greatest two-digit number divided by 20?

6 There are 720 pupils in a school. If they stand in the different numbers of rows as indicated in the table below, how many pupils are there in each row? Fill in the table with your answers.

Number of rows	10	20	30	40	60	80
Number of pupils in each row						

Challenge and extension question

7 (a) Subtract a whole tens number from 480, and then divide the difference by the whole tens number. The quotient is 5. This whole tens number is _____.

(b) In a long distance run, Alvin was 70 metres ahead of Peter. Simon was 40 metres behind Laura. Peter was 30 metres ahead of Simon. The first runner was _____ and the third runner was _____.

(c) When a dividend is divided by a divisor, the quotient is 7 and the remainder is 3. If the sum of the divisor, the dividend, the quotient and the remainder is 85, then the dividend is _____.

(d) Two houses are 250 metres apart. Mr. Wood planted 49 trees with equal distance between them. There are _____ metres between each tree.

3.7 Practice and exercise

Learning objective

Use different methods to multiply and divide three-digit numbers and two-digit numbers

Basic questions

1 Work these out mentally, and then write the answers.

$16 \times 30 =$ $34 \times 5 \div 10 =$ $11 \times 11 \times 0 =$ $4800 \div 20 =$

$72 \times 5 - 20 =$ $100 \div 20 + 100 =$

$9 \times ($ $) = 9090$ $1000 \div ($ $) = 125$

2 Use the column method to calculate. (Check the answer to the question marked with $*$.)

$567 \times 11 =$ $313 \times 32 =$

$2030 \times 420 =$ $* 2551 \div 30 =$

3 Work these out step by step. (Calculate smartly when possible.)

$77 \times 101 + 33$ $46 \times 64 - 64 \times 36$ $432 \times 15 \div 20$ $3200 \div 40 \div 8$

4 Write the number sentences and then calculate.

(a) A is 480 and it is 6 times B. What is the sum of A and B?

(b) The sum of 565 and 19 is divided by 50. What is the quotient?

5 Fill in the blanks.

(a) Split the same multiplication sentence in different ways.

25×36 25×36 25×36

= _____   = _____   = _____

= _____   = _____   = _____

= _____   = _____   = _____

(b) Subtract 80 from 425 for (   ) times so finally there is 25 remaining.

(c) When calculating 25×33, Alvin mistook one of the two 3s for a different number. As a result, the product is 50 greater than the correct answer. Alvin mistook 33 for (   ).

(d) $720 \div 60 = 720 \div 6 \div ($ $) = ($ $) \div ($ $) = ($ $)$

(e) When the quotient of $440 \div \boxed{}0$ is a two-digit number, the greatest possible number in the $\boxed{}$ is (   ).

Challenge and extension questions

6 Tom mistook $\star \div 50$ for $\star \div 500$, and therefore he got the quotient 12.

(a) What should the correct quotient be?

(b) How much does $\star$ stand for?

7 A circular pond has a perimeter of 300 metres. If a willow tree is planted every 5 metres, how many willow trees are needed?

Unit test 3

1 Work these out mentally, and then write the answers.

$125 \times 4 =$	$111 \times 30 =$	$950 \div 20 =$	$300 \div 30 =$
$240 \times 40 =$	$8 \times 125 =$	$2500 \div 50 =$	$4900 \div 70 =$
$3 \times 125 =$	$121 \div 11 =$	$5 \times 5 \times 50 =$	$144 \div 12 \div 2 =$

2 Use the column method to calculate. (Check the answer to the last question in each row.)

(a) $207 \times 43 =$ (b) $880 \times 2300 =$ (c) $492 \times 20 =$

(d) $416 \times 47 =$ (e) $4256 \div 30 =$ (f) $16\,919 \div 50 =$

3 Work these out step by step. (Calculate smartly when possible.)

(a) $2623 - 1746 + 1377$ (b) $203 \times 15 + 85$

(c) $45 \times 235 - 45 \times 135$ (d) $909 \times 20 \div 10$

(e) $2400 \div 20 \div 4$ (f) $39 \times (100 - 25)$

4 Fill in the brackets.

(a) The product of 8500×160 has (   ) zeros at the end.

(b) The sum of the least three-digit number and the greatest three-digit number is (   ).

(c) The quotient of $5000 \div 50$ is a (   )-digit number. The highest value place of the quotient is in the (   ) place. There are (   ) zeros at the end of the quotient.

(d) In $60\overline{)\ \boxed{}\ 2\ 6\ 5}$, if the quotient is a three-digit number, the least possible number in the $\boxed{}$ is (   ). If the quotient is a two-digit number, the number in the $\boxed{}$ could be (   ).

(e) To saw a 125-metre-long log into 5 pieces, it needs to be sawn (   ) times.

5 Multiple choice questions.

(a) To calculate 31×29, the wrong method in the following is (   ).

   A. $31 \times 30 - 31 \times 1$ B. $31 \times 20 + 31 \times 9$

   C. $30 \times 29 + 29$ D. $(31 - 1) \times (29 + 1)$

(b) 99 is divided by a number, and the quotient is a one-digit number. What is the least possible number of the divisor? (   )

   A. 100   B. 99   C. 10   D. 11

(c) A three-digit number is multiplied by a two-digit number, the product is a (   )-digit number.

   A. six   B. five   C. five or four   D. Not sure

(d) James and Simon are living in the same apartment building. James is living on the fifth floor, and Simon is living on the second floor. The number of steps between neighbouring floors is the same. If Simon needs to walk 36 steps from the ground floor to his home, then James needs to walk (   ) steps from the ground floor to his home.

   A. 72   B. 90   C. 108   D. 120

6 Application problems.

(a) In a supermarket, eggs are packed in cartons with each holding 12 eggs. A box contains 10 cartons of eggs. A canteen bought 12 boxes of eggs. How many eggs did it buy? If the canteen uses 80 eggs a day, how many days can these eggs last?

(b) A fruit shop received a delivery of 3680 kilograms of watermelon in the morning. It was half of the weight delivered in the afternoon. How many kilograms of watermelon did the shop receive in total on that day?

(c) The pumping machine in a construction site pumped 730 tons of water during the day and 350 tons at night. If it works 20 hours in the whole day, how much water did it pump every hour on average?

(d)

£10   £85

A shop purchased 100 pieces each of the normal Rubik's cubes and Irregular Rubik's cubes as shown in the diagram. After having sold out of all the cubes, it made profit of £200 from the sale of the normal Rubik's cubes and £500 from the sale of the Irregular Rubik's cubes. What prices did the shop pay for the two types of cubes, respectively?

Chapter 4 Addition and subtraction of fractions

4.1 Fractions in hundredths

 Learning objective

Recognise and use hundredths

 Basic questions

1. Fill in each bracket with a fraction.
   (a) If a whole is divided into 2 equal parts, each part is (   ) of the whole.
   (b) If a whole is divided into 10 equal parts, 3 parts are (   ) of the whole.
   (c) If a whole is divided into 100 equal parts, each part is (   ) of the whole.
   (d) If a whole is divided into 200 equal parts, 3 parts are (   ) of the whole.

2. Shade part of each diagram to represent the fraction given. The first has been done for you.

   (a)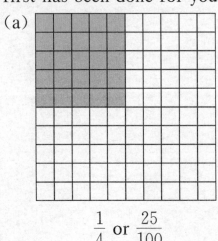

   (b)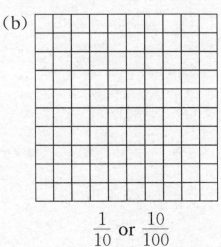

   $\frac{1}{4}$ or $\frac{25}{100}$ $\frac{1}{10}$ or $\frac{10}{100}$

(c)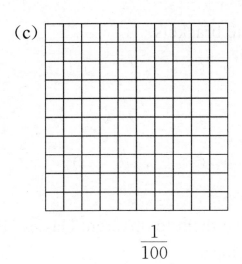

$$\frac{1}{100}$$

(d)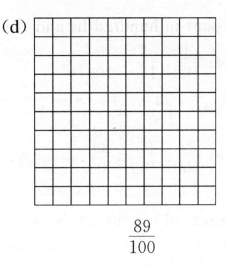

$$\frac{89}{100}$$

3 Circle equivalent fractions and draw lines to link them. One has been done for you.

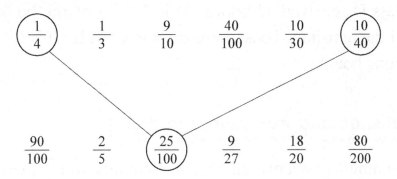

4 Mark the following fractions on the number line.

(a)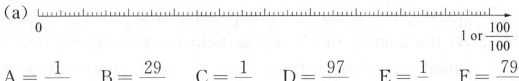

0

1 or $\frac{100}{100}$

$A = \frac{1}{100}$ $B = \frac{29}{100}$ $C = \frac{1}{10}$ $D = \frac{97}{100}$ $E = \frac{1}{2}$ $F = \frac{79}{100}$

(b)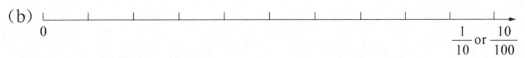

0

$\frac{1}{10}$ or $\frac{10}{100}$

$A = \frac{1}{100}$ $B = \frac{3}{100}$ $C = \frac{7}{10}$ $D = \frac{9}{100}$

5 Count in hundredths and fill in the brackets.

(a) $\dfrac{1}{100}$, $\dfrac{3}{100}$, $\dfrac{5}{100}$, (   ), (   ), (   ), (   )

(b) 0, $\dfrac{11}{100}$, $\dfrac{21}{100}$, $\dfrac{31}{100}$, (   ), (   ), (   ), (   )

(c) $\dfrac{97}{100}$, $\dfrac{93}{100}$, $\dfrac{89}{100}$, (   ), (   ), (   ), (   )

6 A school bought 200 books and gave them to different classes. Fill in the brackets with suitable fractions.

(a) Class A received 20 books. It is (   ) of the books bought.

(b) Class B received 38 books. It is (   ) of the books bought.

(c) Class C received 60 books. It is (   ) of the books bought.

(d) Class D received 42 books. It is (   ) of the books bought.

(e) All the remaining books were given to Class E. It is (   ) of the books bought.

Challenge and extension question

7 In a community event, all the participants were divided into 10 equal groups. The participants in the first group were further divided into 10 equal subgroups. Answer the following:

(a) What fraction of all the participants was the number of the participants in each subgroup of the first group?

(b) If the number of all the participants was exactly 500, how many participants were there in each group? How many participants were there in each subgroup of the first group?

4.2 Addition and subtraction of fractions (1)

 Learning objective

Add fractions with the same denominator

Basic questions (1)

1. Think carefully. Fill in the brackets and calculate.

(a) $\dfrac{3}{10} + \dfrac{4}{10} = \dfrac{3+4}{10} = \dfrac{(\quad)}{10}$

We can also calculate this way: adding ( ) lots of $\dfrac{1}{10}$ and

( ) lots of $\dfrac{1}{10}$, the sum is ( ) lots of $\dfrac{1}{10}$, which is

(—). We can represent the addition using the diagram

below. (Can you use another way to represent this?)

$$\dfrac{3}{10} + \dfrac{4}{10} = \dfrac{(\quad)}{(\quad)}$$

| $\frac{1}{10}$ | $\frac{1}{10}$ | $\frac{1}{10}$ | $\frac{1}{10}$ | $\frac{1}{10}$ | $\frac{1}{10}$ | $\frac{1}{10}$ | | | |

$$\underbrace{\qquad}_{\frac{3}{10}} \quad \underbrace{\qquad}_{\frac{4}{10}}$$

(b) $\dfrac{7}{17} + \dfrac{9}{17} = \dfrac{7+9}{17} = \dfrac{(\quad)}{17}$

We can also calculate this way: adding ( ) lots of $\dfrac{1}{17}$ and

( ) lots of $\dfrac{1}{17}$, the sum is ( ) lots of $\dfrac{1}{17}$, which is

( ) Can you draw a diagram to represent $\dfrac{7}{17} + \dfrac{9}{17}$?

(c) In general, adding fractions with the same denominator means ( ) the numerators and keeping the denominator ( ).

2 Calculate.

(a) $\dfrac{1}{7} + \dfrac{3}{7} = ($ $)$ (b) $\dfrac{2}{5} + \dfrac{1}{5} = ($ $)$

(c) $\dfrac{9}{20} + \dfrac{4}{20} = ($ $)$ (d) $\dfrac{6}{43} + \dfrac{16}{43} = ($ $)$

(e) $\dfrac{50}{77} + \dfrac{10}{77} = ($ $)$ (f) $\dfrac{115}{800} + \dfrac{345}{800} = ($ $)$

(g) $\dfrac{3}{9} + \dfrac{4}{9} + \dfrac{1}{9} = ($ $)$ (h) $\dfrac{5}{32} + \dfrac{6}{32} + \dfrac{7}{32} + \dfrac{8}{32} = ($ $)$

3 Fill in the blanks.

(a) (   ) lots of $\dfrac{1}{15}$ are $\dfrac{13}{15}$. 8 lots of $\dfrac{1}{9}$ are (   ).

(b) 5 lots of $\dfrac{1}{6}$ are (   ). Adding it to 1 lot of $\dfrac{1}{6}$ is (   ).

(c) There is a pile of rubbers. Four of them are red, which is $\dfrac{4}{11}$ of the whole pile. If we add one more red rubber, then the red rubbers are (   ) of the whole pile.

4 Write the number sentences and then calculate.

(a) What is the sum of 5 lots of $\dfrac{1}{20}$ and 7 lots of $\dfrac{1}{20}$?

(b) After $\dfrac{3}{19}$ is taken away from a number, the result is $\dfrac{11}{19}$. Find the number.

⑤ In an auto rally, the Drucker team drove $\frac{3}{10}$ of the whole journey on the first day. On the second day, they drove $\frac{4}{10}$ of the whole journey and on the third day they drove $\frac{2}{10}$ of the journey. Using a fraction, how much of the journey did the team drive in the first three days?

 Challenge and extension questions

⑥ Write a suitable fraction or a number in each bracket.

(a) $\frac{3}{10} + (\quad) = \frac{1}{2}$　　　　　(b) $\frac{3}{10} + (\quad) = 1$

(c) $\frac{9}{22} + (\quad) = \frac{1}{2}$　　　　　(d) $\frac{20}{24} = \frac{(\quad)}{48} = \frac{5}{(\quad)}$

⑦ Look for patterns and then fill in the ☐ with a suitable number.

$\frac{1}{2} = \frac{1}{3} + \frac{1}{6}, \frac{1}{3} = \frac{1}{4} + \frac{1}{12}, \frac{1}{4} = \frac{1}{5} + \frac{1}{20}$

$\frac{1}{5} = \frac{1}{\square} + \frac{1}{\square}, \frac{1}{9} = \frac{1}{\square} + \frac{1}{\square}, \frac{1}{50} = \frac{1}{\square} + \frac{1}{\square}$

4.3   Addition and subtraction of fractions (2)

 Learning objective

Subtract fractions with the same denominator

 Basic questions

1 Think carefully. Fill in the brackets and calculate.

(a) $\dfrac{9}{10} - \dfrac{3}{10} = \dfrac{9-3}{10} = \dfrac{(\quad)}{10}$

We can also calculate this way: (   ) lots of $\dfrac{1}{10}$ minus

(   ) lots of $\dfrac{1}{10}$, the difference is (   ) lots of $\dfrac{1}{10}$, which is

(—). We can represent the subtraction using the diagram
below. (Can you use another way to represent this?)

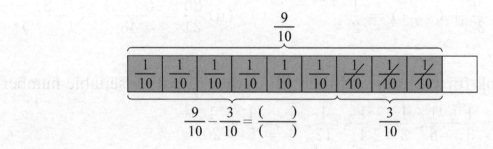

(b) $\dfrac{16}{17} - \dfrac{9}{17} = \dfrac{16-9}{17} = \dfrac{(\quad)}{17}$

or you can calculate this way: (   ) lots of $\dfrac{1}{17}$ minus (   )

lots of $\dfrac{1}{17}$, the difference is (—). Can you draw a diagram to

represent $\dfrac{16}{17} - \dfrac{9}{17}$?

(c) In general, subtracting fractions with the same denominator means (　　) the numerators and keeping the denominators (　　).

2 Calculate.

(a) $\dfrac{5}{6} - \dfrac{4}{6} = (—)$

(b) $\dfrac{9}{14} - \dfrac{3}{14} = (—)$

(c) $\dfrac{17}{30} - \dfrac{8}{30} = (—)$

(d) $\dfrac{29}{72} - \dfrac{16}{72} = (—)$

(e) $\dfrac{90}{300} - \dfrac{40}{300} = (—)$

(f) $\dfrac{8}{25} - \dfrac{6}{25} = (—)$

(g) $1 - \dfrac{8}{65} - \dfrac{9}{65} - \dfrac{10}{65} = (—)$

(h) $\dfrac{(\quad)}{36} - \dfrac{10}{36} = \dfrac{11}{36}$

(i) $\dfrac{10}{100} - \dfrac{(\quad)}{100} = \dfrac{3}{100}$

3 Write the number sentences and then calculate.

(a) After taking away $\dfrac{3}{15}$ from a minuend, the result is $\dfrac{11}{15}$. Find the minuend.

(b) What is the result of taking away 4 lots of $\dfrac{1}{20}$ from $\dfrac{8}{20}$?

(c) What is the difference of subtracting 3 lots of $\dfrac{1}{7}$ from 1?

Challenge and extension questions

4 Let's calculate.

(a) $\dfrac{4}{9} + \dfrac{5}{9} - \dfrac{9}{10}$

(b) $1 - \dfrac{10}{10} + \dfrac{9}{10}$

(c) $\dfrac{7}{12} + \dfrac{5}{9} + \dfrac{5}{12} + \dfrac{4}{9}$

(d) $1 - \dfrac{1}{5} - \dfrac{3}{8} + \dfrac{1}{5}$

5 At Shirley's birthday, Dad gave $\dfrac{3}{4}$ of the cake to Grandpa, Grandma, Aunt and Cousin. Shirley and Mum had $\dfrac{1}{8}$ of the cake each. Was there any cake left for Dad himself?

4.4 Fun with exploration — 'fraction wall'

Learning objective

Compare, add and subtract fractions

Basic questions

1. Learning buddy — 'fraction wall'.
   Look at the fraction wall below. What do you notice?

1															
$\frac{1}{2}$								$\frac{1}{2}$							
$\frac{1}{3}$				$\frac{1}{3}$					$\frac{1}{3}$						
$\frac{1}{4}$			$\frac{1}{4}$				$\frac{1}{4}$				$\frac{1}{4}$				
$\frac{1}{5}$		$\frac{1}{5}$			$\frac{1}{5}$			$\frac{1}{5}$			$\frac{1}{5}$				
$\frac{1}{6}$		$\frac{1}{6}$		$\frac{1}{6}$		$\frac{1}{6}$		$\frac{1}{6}$		$\frac{1}{6}$					
$\frac{1}{7}$		$\frac{1}{7}$		$\frac{1}{7}$		$\frac{1}{7}$		$\frac{1}{7}$		$\frac{1}{7}$		$\frac{1}{7}$			
$\frac{1}{8}$	$\frac{1}{8}$		$\frac{1}{8}$		$\frac{1}{8}$		$\frac{1}{8}$		$\frac{1}{8}$		$\frac{1}{8}$		$\frac{1}{8}$		
$\frac{1}{9}$	$\frac{1}{9}$	$\frac{1}{9}$		$\frac{1}{9}$		$\frac{1}{9}$		$\frac{1}{9}$		$\frac{1}{9}$		$\frac{1}{9}$		$\frac{1}{9}$	
$\frac{1}{10}$	$\frac{1}{10}$	$\frac{1}{10}$	$\frac{1}{10}$		$\frac{1}{10}$		$\frac{1}{10}$		$\frac{1}{10}$		$\frac{1}{10}$	$\frac{1}{10}$		$\frac{1}{10}$	
$\frac{1}{12}$	$\frac{1}{12}$	$\frac{1}{12}$	$\frac{1}{12}$	$\frac{1}{12}$	$\frac{1}{12}$	$\frac{1}{12}$	$\frac{1}{12}$	$\frac{1}{12}$	$\frac{1}{12}$	$\frac{1}{12}$	$\frac{1}{12}$				
$\frac{1}{16}$	$\frac{1}{16}$	$\frac{1}{16}$	$\frac{1}{16}$	$\frac{1}{16}$	$\frac{1}{16}$	$\frac{1}{16}$	$\frac{1}{16}$	$\frac{1}{16}$	$\frac{1}{16}$	$\frac{1}{16}$	$\frac{1}{16}$	$\frac{1}{16}$	$\frac{1}{16}$	$\frac{1}{16}$	$\frac{1}{16}$

The fraction wall is very helpful in comparing fractions with the same denominators or the same numerators. They make it much easier to see the two fractions to be compared, making the comparison straightforward.

A fraction wall can also help us visualise the addition and subtraction of fractions with the same denominators.

Drawing a vertical line from the top to the bottom in a fraction wall can help us quickly find the equal fractions.

2 Compare the fractions using the fraction wall above and fill in the boxes with $>$, $<$ or $=$.

(a) $\dfrac{5}{12}$ ☐ $\dfrac{8}{12}$ (b) $\dfrac{7}{9}$ ☐ $\dfrac{4}{9}$ (c) $\dfrac{1}{10}$ ☐ $\dfrac{3}{10}$

(d) $\dfrac{4}{8}$ ☐ $\dfrac{1}{2}$ (e) $\dfrac{7}{16}$ ☐ $\dfrac{7}{10}$ (f) $\dfrac{10}{12}$ ☐ $\dfrac{10}{16}$

3 Do the calculation first, and then check your answers using the fraction wall above.

(a) $\dfrac{1}{9} + \dfrac{8}{9} =$ (b) $\dfrac{11}{12} - \dfrac{9}{12} =$ (c) $\dfrac{1}{7} + \dfrac{2}{7} + \dfrac{3}{7} =$

4 Find out $\dfrac{4}{6}$, $\dfrac{2}{3}$, $\dfrac{3}{4}$ and $\dfrac{1}{4}$ in the fraction wall above.

(a) The fractions that are same as $\dfrac{4}{6}$ are _____ .

(b) The fractions that are same as $\dfrac{2}{3}$ are _____ .

(c) The fractions that are same as $\dfrac{3}{4}$ are _____ .

(d) The fractions that are same as $\dfrac{1}{4}$ are _____ .

Challenge and extension question

5 Fun with the subtraction of fractions.

Do the following: Take away half $\left(\dfrac{1}{2}\right)$ from 1, and then take way

half $\left(\dfrac{1}{4}\right)$ from $\dfrac{1}{2}$ and again take away half $\left(\dfrac{1}{8}\right)$ from $\dfrac{1}{4}$, and then

continue to take away half $\left(\dfrac{1}{16}\right)$ from $\dfrac{1}{8}$ ......

The calculation is a bit challenging, but after you get the result you will find something interesting.

Try the following on your own and write the result.

$$1 - \frac{1}{2} - \frac{1}{4} - \frac{1}{8} - \frac{1}{16} =$$

Unit test 4

1 Work these out mentally, and then write the answers.

(a) $7 \times 11 + 7 =$ (b) $56 \div 8 \times 9 =$ (c) $60 \div 30 + 34 =$

(d) $200 \div 5 \times 8 =$ (e) $12 \times 50 - 100 =$ (f) $180 - 99 + 1 =$

(g) $\frac{2}{7} + \frac{1}{7} =$ (h) $\frac{6}{23} + \frac{17}{23} =$ (i) $(\quad) + \frac{1}{16} = \frac{9}{16}$

(j) $1 - \frac{7}{13} =$ (k) $\frac{4}{5} - \frac{1}{5} =$ (l) $(\quad) - \frac{3}{16} = \frac{1}{2}$

2 Work these out step by step.

(a) $\frac{1}{8} + \frac{3}{8} + \frac{2}{8}$ (b) $\frac{10}{11} - \frac{7}{11} - \frac{1}{11}$ (c) $\frac{3}{14} + \frac{5}{14} - \frac{4}{14}$

(d) $\frac{12}{25} - \frac{4}{25} + \frac{9}{25}$ (e) $\frac{7}{9} + \frac{2}{9} - \frac{31}{74}$ (f) $\frac{5}{14} - \frac{7}{14} + \frac{6}{14}$

3 Shade part of each diagram to represent the fraction given.

(a)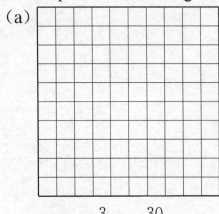

(b)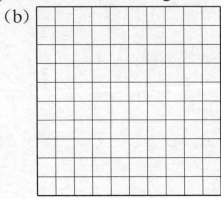

$\frac{3}{10}$ or $\frac{30}{100}$

$\frac{77}{100}$

4 Fill in the brackets.

(a) $\dfrac{3}{8}=\dfrac{(\quad)}{16}=\dfrac{12}{(\quad)}$

(b) $\dfrac{1}{5}=\dfrac{(\quad)}{10}=\dfrac{(\quad)}{100}$

(c) (　) lots of $\dfrac{1}{5}$ makes 1.　(d) 50 lots of $\dfrac{1}{100}$ makes (　).

(e) (　) lots of (　) is $\dfrac{7}{11}$.　(f) $\dfrac{1}{10}$ divided by 10 makes (　).

(g) Adding (　) lots of $\dfrac{1}{18}$ to $\dfrac{13}{18}$, the result equals 1. Taking

away (　) lots of $\dfrac{1}{18}$ from $\dfrac{13}{18}$, the result equals $\dfrac{1}{2}$.

5 Multiple choice questions.

(a) Fold a rope in half twice, and then fold it in half one more time. Now each part is (　) of the whole.

A. $\dfrac{1}{2}$　　B. $\dfrac{1}{4}$　　C. $\dfrac{1}{8}$　　D. $\dfrac{1}{16}$

(b) The incorrect statement of the following is (　).

A. Dividing a square into 100 equal parts, each part is $\dfrac{1}{100}$ of the whole.

B. Dividing one tenth of a square by 100, each part is $\dfrac{1}{100}$ of the whole.

C. Dividing one tenth of a square by 10, each part is $\dfrac{1}{100}$ of the whole.

D. Dividing half of a square by 50, each part is $\dfrac{1}{100}$ of the whole.

6 Write the number sentences and then calculate.

(a) How much greater is $\frac{4}{5}$ than $\frac{1}{5}$?

(b) What is the result of $\frac{79}{80}$ minus $\frac{50}{80}$ and then plus $\frac{30}{80}$?

7 Application problems.

(a) The new school term is around the corner. The staff from a bookshop plan to deliver books for children. A van can load 1200 books per trip. How many books can be delivered by four vans for two trips?

(b) A bundle of pencils were shared among four children. Michelle got 4 pencils, Mary got 5 pencils, John got 6 pencils and Tom got 7 pencils. What fraction of the total pencils did Mary get?

(c) A box of tea weighs 1 kilogram. How many grams of tea were left after $\frac{1}{4}$ of the tea was taken from the box?

Chapter 5 Consolidation and enhancement

5.1 Multiplication and multiplication table

 Learning objective

Recall multiplication facts and solve multiplication problems

 Basic questions

1 Complete the multiplication table of 12×12.

$\times$	1	2	3	4	5	6	7	8	9	10	11	12
1		2										
2			6									
3				12								
4					20							
5						30						
6							42					
7								56				
8									72			
9										90		
10											110	
11												132
12	12											

2 Fill in the brackets and write two multiplication sentences and two division sentences accordingly.

(a) 7 times 8 is (   ).   (b) 8 times 11 is (   ).   (c) 5 times 12 is (   )

_____   _____   _____

_____   _____   _____

_____   _____   _____

_____   _____   _____

(d) 6 times (   ) is 60.   (e) (   ) times 9 is 72.   (f) (   ) times 12 is 1:

_____   _____   _____

_____   _____   _____

_____   _____   _____

_____   _____   _____

3 Represent the following repeated additions as multiplications and then write the answers.

(a) $3+3+3+3 = ($ $) \times ($ $) = ($ $)$

(b) $6+6+6+6+6+6+6+6+6 = ($ $) \times ($ $) = ($ $)$

(c) $11+11+11+11+11+11 = ($ $) \times ($ $) = ($ $)$

(d) $7+7+7+7+7 = ($ $) \times ($ $) = ($ $)$

(e) $12+12+12+12+12+12+12+12 = ($ $) \times ($ $) =$

(   )

4 A new school enrolled 40 students in the first year. In the second year, enrolment doubled, and in the third year it tripled. What was the enrolment in the second year? What was the enrolment in the third year? Write the number sentences and find the answers.

5 Solve the following multiplication problems.

(a) There are three T-shirts and four pairs of trousers. Each T-shirt can be matched with any of the trousers. How many different outfits can these T-shirts and trousers match up?

(b) A pub serves four choices of burgers — beef, chicken, fish and vegetarian, and five choices of drinks — juice, coffee, cola, water and chocolate. Jane wants one burger and one drink. How many different combinations can she have?

 Challenge and extension questions

6 There are two roads from Place A to Place B, three roads from Place B to Place C and two roads from Place C to Place D. How many different ways can one travel by road from Place A to Place D, passing through Place B and then Place C?

7 Two chess pieces are to be placed in two cells of the grid paper below. If they should be laid in neither the same row nor the same column, how many different ways can these two chess pieces be laid?

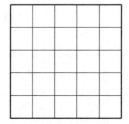

5.2 Relationship between addition and subtraction

Learning objective

Use the inverse relationship between addition and subtraction

Basic questions

1 Fill in the brackets.

(a) (i)
$$50 + 80 = (\quad)$$
$$(\quad) + 80 = 130$$
$$130 - 80 = (\quad)$$

(ii)
$$53 + 47 = (\quad)$$
$$47 + (\quad) = 100$$
$$100 - (\quad) = (\quad)$$

(iii)
$$230 - 70 = (\quad)$$
$$70 + (\quad) = 230$$
$$(\quad) - 160 = 70$$

(iv)
$$190 - 90 = (\quad)$$
$$190 - (\quad) = 90$$
$$(\quad) - 90 = (\quad) + 10$$

(b) Addend = (   ) − Addend   Minuend − Subtrahend = (   )

Subtrahend = Minuend − (   )   (   ) = Difference + Subtrahend

Subtraction is the inverse operation of (   ).

2 Use the relationship between addition and subtraction to complete the following number sentences.

(a) $419 + 363 = 782$

$782 \bigcirc 363 = 419$

$782 \bigcirc 419 = 363$

(b) $1950 - 1016 = 934$

$1950 \bigcirc 934 = 1016$

$1016 \bigcirc 934 = 1950$

(c) $756 + 112 = 868$

$112 = \underline{\hspace{2cm}}$

$756 = \underline{\hspace{2cm}}$

(d) $\square - \bigcirc = \triangle$

$\square = \underline{\hspace{2cm}}$

$\bigcirc = \underline{\hspace{2cm}}$

3 Find the number in the ☐. Show your working. The first one has been done for you.

(a) $165 - \boxed{} = 88$

$\boxed{} = 165 - 88$

$= 77$

(b) $76 + \boxed{} = 311$

(c) $\boxed{} + 901 = 1002$

(d) $\boxed{} - 190 = 75$

4 Write the number sentences and then calculate.

(a) An addend is 126. The sum of this addend and the other addend is 789. Find the other addend.

(b) The minuend is 120 and the difference is half of the minuend. Find the subtrahend.

Challenge and extension questions

5 True or false.

(a) If $A - 139 = 1080$, then $A = 1080 - 139$.   (   )

(b) In a subtraction sentence, if the subtrahend equals the difference, the minuend must be twice the difference.   (   )

6 Tom made a careless mistake when he was working on an addition sentence. He mistakenly wrote an addend, 36, as 63 and therefore, the sum was 278. What is the other addend?

5.3 Relationship between multiplication and division

 Learning objective

Use the inverse relationship between multiplication and division

 Basic questions

1 Fill in the brackets.

(a) (i)
| $22 \times 5 = ($ $)$ |
| $($ $) \times 5 = 110$ |
| $110 \div ($ $) = 5$ |

(ii)
| $120 \div 10 = ($ $)$ |
| $12 \times 10 = ($ $)$ |
| $120 = ($ $) \times 10$ |

(iii)
| $125 \times 8 = ($ $)$ |
| $1000 = ($ $) \times 125$ |
| $($ $) \times 8 = 1000$ |

(iv)
| $35 \times 4 = ($ $)$ |
| $4 \times ($ $) = 140$ |
| $140 \div 4 = ($ $)$ |

(b) Factor $= ($ $) \div$ Factor

     $($ $) =$ Quotient $\times$ Divisor   Dividend $\div ($ $) =$ Divisor

(c) Put a $\checkmark$ in the brackets for the correct answer.

The product of multiplication is equivalent to which term of

its related division
$\begin{cases} \text{dividend } (\quad) \\ \text{divisor } (\quad) \\ \text{quotient } (\quad) \end{cases}$

2 Find the number in the ▭. Show your working. The first one has been done for you.

(a) $15 \times \boxed{} = 150$

     $\boxed{} = 150 \div 15$

     $= 10$

(b) $960 \div \boxed{} = 80$

(c) $\boxed{} \div 9 = 12$

(d) $\boxed{} \times 70 = 1050$

(e) □ × 21 = 189   (f) 2800 − □ = 40

3 Write the number sentences and then calculate.

(a) A factor is 8. When multiplied by the other factor, the product is 768. Find the other factor. (Hint: make a guess first.)

(b) The dividend is 288. The quotient and the remainder are 2 and 4 respectively. Find the divisor.

(c) 840 is 30 times a number. What is the number?

 Challenge and extension questions

4 When Lily was multiplying two numbers, she misread a factor '32' as '30', and got the product as 360. Think carefully and find the correct product.

5 A number can be exactly divided by another number and the quotient is 9. The sum of the dividend and divisor is 210. What are the dividend and divisor? (Hint: make a guess first.)

5.4 Multiplication by two-digit numbers

 Learning objective

Use written methods to multiply by two-digit numbers

 Basic questions

1 Work these out mentally, and then write the answers.

$220 \times 4 =$	$900 \div 20 =$	$25 \times 30 =$
$1200 \div 40 =$	$8100 \div 90 =$	$102 \times 20 =$
$60 \div 30 =$	$700 \div 35 =$	$30 \times 12 =$
$220 \div 11 =$	$42 \times 4 =$	$800 \div 50 =$

2 Use the column method to calculate. (Check the answers to the questions marked with $*$.)

(a) $48 \times 126 =$ (b) $^* 2610 \div 30 =$ (c) $^* 270 \times 60 =$

3 Use the four digits 8, 4, 2 and 5 to make a multiplication of two two-digit numbers. What is the greatest possible product? What is the least possible product? Write the number sentences and then calculate.

4 In 2014, Mary's family saved on average £25 per month on the water bill and £19 per month on the electricity bill. How much did they save on the water and electricity bills for the whole year?

5 A school paid £9720 for electricity for the year of 2014. In response to an energy-saving campaign, the school launched an 'electricity-saving' plan in 2015, aiming to save £90 per month compared with the year of 2014. According to this plan, how much would the school pay for the electricity bill in 2015?

Challenge and extension questions

6 Fill in the brackets.

(a) In multiplying 914×62, the product of the digit '9' and the digit '6' is the same as (   ) $\times$ (   ).

(b) The product of 27×42 is a (   )-digit number. It is between (   ) and (   ), nearer to (   ).

(c) There are (   ) zeros at the end of the product of 25×800.

7 Fill in the boxes and complete the following.

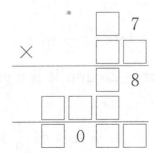

5.5 Practice with fractions

Learning objective

Calculate fractions of amounts and add and subtract fractions

Basic questions

1 Use fractions to represent the shaded parts.

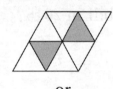  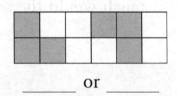

_____ or _____   _____ or _____   _____ or _____

2 Colour $\frac{1}{4}$ of the whole figure in each figure.

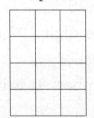   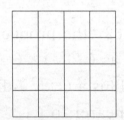   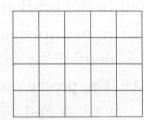

3 Fill in the brackets.

(a) Dividing a pizza into 12 equal pieces, each piece is (   ) of the whole.

(b) There are (   ) lots of $\frac{1}{6}$ in 1.

(c) The denominator is 23 and it is 6 greater than the numerator. The fraction is (   ).

(d) 5 lots of $\frac{1}{6}$ is (   ). 8 lots of $\frac{1}{9}$ is (   ).

(e) $\frac{7}{11}$ consists of (   ) lots of $\frac{1}{11}$.

(f) (   ) lots of $\frac{1}{4}$ equals 1.

(g) There were 8 sweets. If $\frac{1}{4}$ of them had been eaten, then it means that (   ) sweets had been eaten.

(h) $\frac{1}{2}$ of 18 is (   ). $\frac{2}{3}$ of 12 is (   ).

(i) There are (   ) fractions that are equal to $\frac{2}{3}$.

(j) 4 lots of $\frac{1}{8}$ is equal to (   ) lots of $\frac{1}{10}$.

4 Calculate.

(a) $\frac{1}{4}+\frac{2}{4}$ (b) $\frac{118}{250}-\frac{50}{250}$ (c) $\frac{11}{50}-\frac{7}{50}+\frac{8}{50}$ (d) $1-\frac{5}{7}+\frac{4}{7}$

5 Put these fractions in order, starting with the greatest.

$\frac{99}{100}, \frac{1}{100}, \frac{1}{10}, \frac{1}{2}, \frac{49}{100}$

Challenge and extension question

6 Think carefully, and then fill in the blanks.

(a) A 1-metre-long paper string is cut into 8 equal pieces. The length of each piece is _____ of 1 metre. It is _____ metres long. Five pieces are _____ metres long.

(b) $1-\dfrac{(\quad)}{7}+\dfrac{2}{7}=\dfrac{4}{7}$

(c) $(—)-\dfrac{8}{20}=\dfrac{1}{2}$

(d) $\dfrac{2}{3}=\dfrac{(\quad)}{6}=\dfrac{12}{(\quad)}=\dfrac{18}{(\quad)}=\dfrac{(\quad)}{12}=\dfrac{(\quad)}{24}$

5.6 Roman numerals to 100

Learning objective

Read Roman numerals to 100

Basic questions

1. Read the clocks in Roman numerals and write the times to the nearest minute in the blanks, using the 12-hour format.

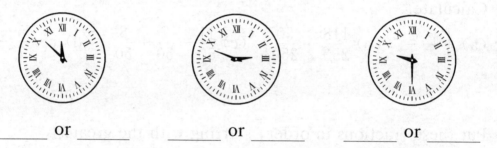

_____ or _____　_____ or _____　_____ or _____

2. Complete the following table in Roman numerals from 1 to 100.

I				V					X
XI			XIV						XX
XXI					XXVI				XXX
XXXI		XXXIII							XL
XLI							XLVIII		L
LI				LV					LX
LXI								LXIX	LXX
LXXI					LXXVI				LXXX
LXXXI	LXXXII								XC
XCI						XCVI			C

3 Match the Roman numerals with the numbers in digits.

(V)   (L)   (I)   (X)   (C)

(100)   (5)   (10)   (50)   (1)

4 Write the following numbers in Roman numerals.

43 =   55 =   12 =   98 =

77 =   60 =   9 =   84 =

5 Write the following Roman numerals in digits.

VI=   LII=   LXXIX=   IX=

XCV=   LXV=   XIX=   LXX=

6 After Sam finished typing three chapters of a book, he found all the pages of these chapters were numbered in Roman numerals starting from I. The first chapter ended at XXIV, the second chapter ended at LIV, and the third chapter ended at LX.

(a) Write the number of pages of each chapter in digits.

(b) How many pages were there in total?

Challenge and extension question

7 True or false.

(a) There is no Roman numeral symbol for the number 0. (   )

(b) Roman numerals cannot represent numbers larger than 100.

(   )

(c) Some Roman numerals are still used today.   (   )

Unit test 5

1 Work these out mentally, and then write the answers.

(a) $77 - 6 - 14 =$ (b) $100 \div 20 + 125 =$ (c) $6 \times 3 \times 10 =$

(d) $44 \times 9 + 44 =$ (e) $12 \times 60 =$ (f) $6 \times 7 + 33 =$

(g) $90 \div 3 - 17 =$ (h) $35 - 35 \div 7 =$ (i) $24 \div 6 \times 8 =$

2 Fill in the boxes.

(a) $\boxed{} + 693 = 8000$ (b) $\boxed{} - 147 = 592$

(c) $82 \times \boxed{} = 738$ (d) $1650 \div \boxed{} = 30$

(e) $\boxed{} \div 103 = 13$ (f) $128 + \boxed{} = 256 - 126$

3 Use the column method to calculate.

(a) $39 \times 102 =$ (b) $385 \times 68 =$ (c) $1080 \div 40 =$

4 Work these out step by step.

(a) $234 \times 55 \div 30$ (b) $36 \times 36 + 36 \times 64$

(c) $(2012 - 162) \div 50$ (d) $398 - 173 - 27 + 112$

5 Calculate.

(a) $\dfrac{11}{15} - \dfrac{4}{15} - \dfrac{7}{15} =$
(b) $\dfrac{26}{35} + \dfrac{9}{35} - \dfrac{11}{35}$
(c) $\dfrac{1}{100} + \dfrac{99}{100} - \dfrac{7}{9}$

6 Write the following Roman numerals in digits.

VI=   XIV=   XCVII=

XLII=   LV=   LXXIX=

7 Fill in the brackets.

(a) When an addition is changed to a subtraction as its (   ) operation, the two addends are equivalent to the (   ) and (   ), and the sum is equivalent to the (   ) in the subtraction.

(b) If the quotient of 960 divided by a number is 30, the number is (   ).

(c) When a number is divided by 80, the quotient is 47. The number is (   ).

(d) When the greatest four-digit number is subtracted by (   ), the result is the greatest three-digit number.

(e) When Lily was doing a division, she mistakenly missed out the zero in the divisor 60, and therefore she got the quotient as 40. The correct quotient should be (   ).

(f) If the difference of 3 ☐ 7 − 257 is a two-digit number, then the greatest possible number in the ☐ should be (   ). If the difference is a three-digit number, then the least possible number in the ☐ should be (   ).

8 Write the number sentences and then calculate.

(a) 220 is subtracted by a number and the difference is 96. Find the number.

(b) The sum of five eights divided by a number is 4. Find the number.

(c) Given that the difference of two numbers is 408, and the subtrahend is 65, what is twice the number of the minuend?

9 Application problems.

(a) John is reading a storybook. He has read 42 pages. The number of pages he has not read yet is five times the number he has read. How many pages has he not read yet?

(b) The sum of the ages of Mary's mother and her grandmother is 100 years. Mary's mother is 38 years old. Mary is 53 years younger than her grandmother. How old are Mary and her grandmother?

(c) In the first half of the year, the school saved £98 on average per month for the water bill and £606 in total for the second half of the year. How much did the school save for the water bill in total in the whole year?

(d) A school bought 36 rubber balls, which was four times the number of footballs the school bought. What is the difference between the number of rubber balls and the number of footballs?

(e) Ming mistakenly wrote the minuend '4' in the ones place as '9', and '0' in the tens place as '6'. Therefore, the difference was 288. What is the correct difference?

(f) Mum bought Tom a green shirt, a blue shirt and a white shirt. She also bought him a pair of leather shoes and a pair of running shoes. In how many combinations can Tom wear his new shirts and shoes?

Chapter 6   Introduction to decimals

6.1   Decimals in life

Learning objective

Recognise decimal numbers in the context of money and measures

Basic questions

1 Read the following information and fill in the blanks below.
In a week in July 2015, the price of unleaded
petrol in a petrol station was 105.7p per litre
and the price of diesel was 112.7p per litre.

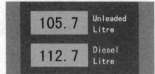

The volume of a soft drink in a bottle sold in
a supermarket is 1.8 litres.

The weight of a bag of peanuts for wild birds
produced by a company is 12.75 kg.

According to Guinness World Records, the tallest human in
recorded history was Robert Wadlow (1918 – 1940), who lived in
the United States. He reached 2.72 m in height.
(a) The decimal numbers used in the above real-life contexts are
    105.7, _____, _____, _____ and _____ .

(Fill in the blanks below with whole numbers.)

(b) The price of unleaded petrol was between _____ pence and _____ pence per litre, closer to _____ pence per litre. The price of diesel was between _____ pence and _____ pence per litre, closer to _____ pence per litre.

(c) The volume of the soft drink is between _____ litres and _____ litres. It is closer to _____ litres.

(d) The weight of peanuts in the bag is between _____ kg and _____ kg. It is closer to _____ kg.

(e) The height Robert Wadlow reached was between _____ m and _____ m. It is closer to _____ m.

2 Read the following prices and fill in the blanks.

Fruit
£13.20

Potato CHIPS
£7.00

Juice Juice Juice Juice Juice Juice Juice
£21.68

(a) £13.20 is _____ pounds and _____ pence.
It is read as _____ pounds.

(b) £7.00 is _____ pounds and _____ pence.
It is read as _____ pounds.

(c) £21.68 is _____ pounds and _____ pence.
It is read as _____ pounds.

Challenge and extension question

3 Martin and Paula had their weight and height measured in the school. Martin said, 'I saw the teacher writing down three numbers 1, 5 and 2 after he measured my height.' What was Martin's height? Paula said, 'I saw the teacher writing down three numbers 3, 4 and 5 to record my weight.' What was Paula's weight?

6.2 Understanding decimals (1)

 Learning objective

Recognise and write decimal equivalents to tenths, hundredths, halves and quarters

 Basic questions

1 Fill in the brackets.

(a)

The shaded part occupies (   ) of the whole.

The unshaded part occupies (   ) of the whole.

The shaded part and the unshaded part added together make a (   ).

(b)

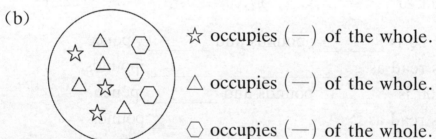

☆ occupies ($\frac{}{}$) of the whole.

△ occupies ($\frac{}{}$) of the whole.

⬡ occupies ($\frac{}{}$) of the whole.

(c) Compare the fractions. Fill in the brackets with $>$, $<$ or $=$.

$\frac{3}{10}$ (   ) $\frac{7}{10}$ $\frac{35}{100}$ (   ) $\frac{3}{100}$ $\frac{303}{1000}$ (   ) $\frac{303}{1000}$

(d) Fill in each bracket below. Use a decimal to represent the fraction or a fraction to represent the decimal.

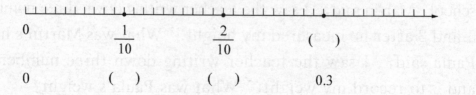

102

(e) All fractions whose denominators are 10, 100 and 1000 etc.
can be expressed as (   ).

$\dfrac{1}{10}$ can be written as a decimal number (   ), it is read as

(   ).

$\dfrac{1}{100}$ can be written as (   ), it is read as (   ).

$\dfrac{1}{1000}$ can be written as (   ), and it is read as (   ).

2 Mark the fractions $\dfrac{1}{4}$, $\dfrac{1}{2}$ and $\dfrac{3}{4}$ on the number line below and then

write their decimal equivalents.

$$\dfrac{1}{4}=\qquad\qquad \dfrac{1}{2}=\qquad\qquad \dfrac{3}{4}=$$

3 Use decimal numbers to express the fractions and read them out.

(a) $\dfrac{7}{10}=$ (b) $\dfrac{16}{100}=$

Read as: _____   Read as: _____

(c) $\dfrac{256}{1000}=$ (d) $\dfrac{8}{10}=$

Read as: _____   Read as: _____

(e) $\dfrac{205}{1000}=$ (f) $\dfrac{95}{100}=$

Read as: _____   Read as: _____

4 Write the following decimals as fractions.

(a) 0.5 = (   )   (b) 0.03 = (   )   (c) 0.24 = (   )

(d) 0.001 = (   )   (e) 0.207 = (   )   (f) 0.9 = (   )

Challenge and extension questions

5 Fill in the brackets. The first one has been done for you as an example.

(a) $\dfrac{3}{10} + \dfrac{4}{10} = (\dfrac{7}{10}) = (0.7)$ It is read as: (zero point seven)

(b) $\dfrac{35}{100} + \dfrac{27}{100} = ($ $) = ($ $)$ It is read as: (   )

(c) $\dfrac{303}{1000} - \dfrac{28}{1000} = ($ $) = ($ $)$ It is read as: (   )

(d) $\dfrac{24}{100} + \dfrac{19}{100} - \dfrac{13}{100} = ($ $) = ($ $)$ It is read as: (   )

6 Simon and Lynn like to drink a brand of milk sold in a 200 ml carton. Simon drank $\dfrac{4}{10}$ of a carton, and Lynn drank $\dfrac{5}{10}$ of another carton. Who has more milk left? How many millilitres did Simon drink? How many millilitres did Lynn drink?

7 Number A and Number B are equal. Number A is $\dfrac{4}{5}$. The denominator of Number B is 10 greater than the denominator of Number A. What is the numerator of Number B?

6.3   Understanding decimals (2)

Learning objective

Recognise and write decimal equivalents to tenths, hundredths and thousandths

Basic questions

1 Complete the following place value chart to represent the decimal number 6735.482.

Whole number part				Decimal point	Decimal part		
Thousands place	Hundreds place	Tens place	Ones place	•	Tenths place	Hundredths place	Thousandths place
		3		•		8	

2 Count in decimals and complete the patterns.
   (a) Count in 0.1s: 0, 0.1, 0.2, 0.3, _____, _____, _____, _____, _____, _____, 1.
   (b) Count in 0.01s: 5.10, 5.11, 5.12, 5.13, _____, _____, _____, _____, _____, _____, 5.20.
   (c) Count back in 0.5s: 10, 9.5, 9.0, 8.5, _____, _____, _____, _____, _____, _____, 5.

3 Think carefully and fill in the brackets.
   (a)

   0.2   (   )   (   )   (   )

   $\frac{1}{10}$ $\frac{3}{10}$ $\frac{5}{10}$ $\frac{7}{10}$ $\frac{9}{10}$ 1

(b) The diagram above shows that $\frac{9}{10}$ is 0.9. If 0.9 is added with one 0.1, we get ten 0.1s, that is (   ).

(c) $\frac{99}{100}$ is 0.99. If 0.99 is added with one 0.01, we get one hundred 0.01s, that is (   ).

$\frac{999}{1000}$ is 0.999. If 0.999 is added with one 0.001, we get one thousand 0.001s, that is (   ).

(d) There are (   ) 0.1s, or (   ) 0.01s, or (   ) 0.001s in 1.

(e) When counting in decimals, 0.1, 0.01, and 0.001 can all be used as units of counting. There are (   ) 0.001s in 0.01, and there are (   ) 0.01s in 0.1.

4 Fill in the brackets.

(a) A decimal number consists of two parts, the (   ) part and the (   ) part.

(b) 0.67 consists of (   ) 0.1s and (   ) 0.01s.

(c) Two 0.1s are (   ). Five 0.01s are (   ). One hundred and twenty-eight 0.001s are (   ).

(d) There are three (   ), nine (   ), one (   ), two (   ) and nine (   ) in 39.129.

(e) In 7.15, '7' is in the (   ) place, representing seven (   ). '1' is in the (   ) place, representing (   ) 0.1. '5' is in the (   ) place, representing five (   ).

5 Multiple choice questions.

(a) A fraction whose denominator is 10 can be written as a decimal with one decimal place. $\frac{5}{10}$ is 0.5, or five (   ).

A. 0.1s   B. 0.01s   C. 0.001s   D. 10s

(b) A fraction whose denominator is 100 can be written as a decimal with two decimal places. $\frac{5}{100}$ is 0.05, or five (   ).

    A. 0.1s   B. 0.01s   C. 0.001s   D. 10s

(c) A fraction with 1000 as the denominator can be written as a decimal with three decimal places. $\frac{5}{1000}$ is 0.005, or five (   ).

    A. 0.1s   B. 0.01s   C. 0.001s   D. 10s

(d) 0.8 equals (   ).

    A. 0.8 thousandths   B. 8 thousandths

    C. 80 thousandths   D. 80 hundredths

Challenge and extension questions

6 Fill in the brackets with decimal numbers.

(a) The number consisting of 65 thousandths is (   ).

(b) In a decimal number, its hundreds place is 6, ones place is 1, hundredths place is 3 and the rest of the places are all zeros. This number is (   ).

(c) A decimal number consists of 4 thousandths and 40 tens. It is (   ).

7 Fiona's average maths test score is a bit more than 93 marks but less than 94. Guess: what could her average maths test score be?

6.4 Understanding decimals (3)

 Learning objective

Recognise and write decimal equivalents to tenths, hundredths and thousandths

 Basic questions

1. Fill in the brackets.

   (a) 2 thousands, 4 tens and 1 tenth make a decimal (   ).

   (b) A number consisting of 143 hundredths is (   ).

   (c) A number consisting of 15 ones and 45 thousandths is (   ).

   (d) Among 0.41, 5.11, 3.03, 0.8 and 1, the mixed decimals are (   );

   > A decimal number whose whole number part is not zero is called a mixed decimal.

   the pure decimals are (   ).

   > A decimal number whose whole number part is zero is called a pure decimal.

   (e) Use 2, 1, 0 and decimal point to make pure decimals with two decimal places. They are (   ).

2. Follow the example given at (a) and fill in the brackets.

   (a) $0.16 = 1 \times 0.1 + 6 \times 0.01$

   (b) $0.448 = (\quad) \times 0.1 + (\quad) \times 0.01 + (\quad) \times 0.001$

   (c) $82.57 = (\quad) \times 10 + (\quad) \times 1 + (\quad) \times 0.1 + (\quad) \times 0.01$

   (d) $0.92 = 9 \times (\quad) + 2 \times (\quad)$

3 True or false.

(a) All decimal numbers are less than 1. ( )

(b) There are thirteen 0.1s in $\dfrac{13}{10}$; it can be written as $\dfrac{13}{10}=1.3$.

( )

(c) $\dfrac{39}{1000}=0.390$. ( )

(d) In a decimal number, the second place to the left of the decimal point is the tens place, while the second place to the right of the decimal point is the tenths place. ( )

(e) 0.99 is the greatest pure decimal number with two decimal places. ( )

(f) 9.99 is the greatest decimal number with two decimal places.

( )

(g) Mixed decimal numbers are always greater than pure decimal numbers. ( )

Challenge and extension question

4 Fill in the brackets.

(a) ( ) consists of 6 hundreds, 3 tens, 9 ones, 1 tenth and 8 hundredths.

(b) The quotient of two numbers in a division is 2. If the dividend is multiplied by 100 and the divisor remains unchanged, then the new quotient is ( ).

(c) Using four digits 1, 2, 6 and 0 and a decimal point to form decimals, the least pure decimal is ( ), the greatest pure decimal is ( ), and the least decimal with two decimal places is ( ).

(d) 0.1 is ( ) times 0.001, while 0.001 is $\dfrac{(\ \ )}{(\ \ )}$ of 0.01.

(e) The greatest decimal with one decimal place, which is less than 1, is (   ); the least decimal with two decimal places, which is greater than 1, is (   ).

(f) In a decimal, the place value of the digit in the tenth place is (   ) times the place value of the same digit in the thousandths place.

6.5 Understanding decimals (4)

Learning objective

Recognise and write decimal equivalents to tenths, hundredths and thousandths

Basic questions

1 Read and write the numbers.

(a) 10.79

Read as: (   ).

(b) 22.023

Read as: (   ).

(c) 9.304

Read as: (   ).

(d) 0.0101

Read as: (   ).

(e) 14.90

Read as: (   ).

(f) 300.303

Read as: (   ).

(g) zero point one seven   Written as: (   ).

(h) sixty point nine eight   Written as: (   ).

(i) twenty point zero zero two   Written as: (   ).

(j) one hundred point three seven five   Written as: (   ).

(k) zero point eight zero six zero   Written as: (   ).

(l) one hundred point nine zero zero   Written as: (   ).

2 Write the decimals into the circles as indicated.

0.9, 54.32, 12.976, 0.31, 46.73, 1.244, 0.18, 9.45, 24.8, 5.77, 7.201, 80.9, 0.07, 100.9.

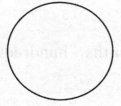
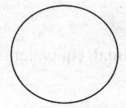
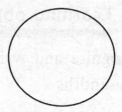

with one decimal place   with two decimal places   with three decimal places

3 Fill in the brackets.

(a) There are (   ) pure decimal numbers with one decimal place. The least one is (   ) and the greatest one is (   ).

(b) There are (   ) pure decimal numbers with two decimal places. The least one is (   ) and the greatest one is (   ).

(c) There are (   ) pure decimal numbers with three decimal places. The least one is (   ) and the greatest one is (   ).

(d) The decimal numbers with two decimal places that come before and after 0.95 are (   ) and (   ).

(e) 40.04 is a decimal with (   ) decimal places. The digit 4 to the right of the decimal point is in the (   ) place. It means (   ). The digit 4 to the left of the decimal point is in the (   ) place. It means (   ). The place value of the digit 4 on the left is (   ) times that of the digit 4 on the right.

4 Use your knowledge to describe decimals.

For example, you can describe 6.78 as follows:

6.78 is a decimal with two decimal places.

6.78 is a mixed decimal.

6.78 consists of 678 hundredths.

6.78 is made of 6 ones, 7 tenths and 8 hundredths.

$6.78 = 6 \times 1 + 7 \times 0.1 + 8 \times 0.01$

Now please try on your own.

(a) 13.5   (b) 0.578

_____   _____

_____   _____

_____   _____

_____   _____

_____   _____

Challenge and extension questions

⑤ Read the following carefully.

For a fraction, if the numerator is equal to the denominator, it can be written as the whole number 1.

If the numerator is less than the denominator, the fraction is called a **proper fraction**. If the numerator is greater than or equal to the denominator, it is called an **improper fraction**.

A proper fraction can be converted to a pure decimal. When a smaller number is divided by a bigger number, the quotient is less than 1, therefore the whole number part of the resulting decimal is zero. Pure decimal numbers are smaller than 1.

An improper fraction can be converted to a mixed decimal. When its numerator is divided by its denominator, the quotient is greater than or equal to 1. Mixed decimal numbers are greater than or equal to 1.

Therefore, a mixed decimal is $\geqslant 1 >$ a pure decimal. (Note: the sign $\geqslant$ means greater than or equal to.)

For example: $1.4 = \dfrac{14}{10} = 1\dfrac{4}{10}$. It is read as one and four tenths,

and considered as: $1 + \dfrac{4}{10}$ or $1 + 0.4$. Have a try on your own:

$1.12 =$ _____ $=$ _____ ; $58.33 =$ _____ $=$ _____ .

6 There is a mixed decimal. Its whole number part is the greatest two-digit number. The digit in the hundredths place is the greatest single digit, and the digit in the tenths place is the least single digit. This mixed decimal is (   ).

6.6 Understanding decimals (5)

Learning objective

Use decimals and convert between different units of measure

Basic questions

1. Write a suitable number in the bracket. (Note: 1 km＝1000 m, 1 m＝100 cm and 1 cm＝10 mm; drawing not to scale)

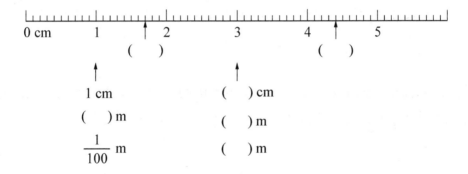

2. Draw lines to match equivalent measures of length.

$\frac{3}{10}$ m   1 cm   90 mm

10 mm   0.3 m $\frac{7}{10}$ cm

9 cm   0.7 cm   30 cm

7 mm   0.09 m   0.01 m

3 Use decimals to represent the lengths of the objects below.

(a)

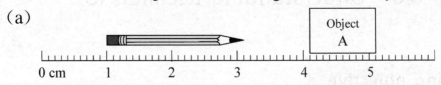

The length of the pencil: (   )   The length of Object A: (   )

(b)

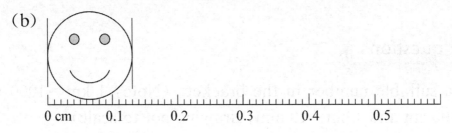

The length of the smiley face eraser: (   )

4 Use a ruler to measure the length of each side of the triangle and find the perimeter of the triangle. (Unit: cm)

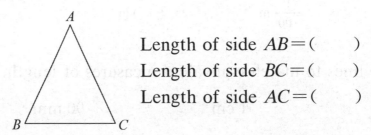

Length of side $AB=$ (   )
Length of side $BC=$ (   )
Length of side $AC=$ (   )

The perimeter of the triangle is: _____

Challenge and extension questions

5 Grandma drank 50 ml more than half of a bottle of milk. There were 530 ml of milk remaining in the bottle. How much milk did the bottle contain?

6 Fill in the brackets.

(a) 60 cm expressed using a fraction is (   ) m, and using a decimal is (   ) m. Eight mm expressed using a fraction is (   ) m, and using a decimal is (   ) m.

(b) A number made up of 3 thousands, 4 ones, 9 hundredths and 8 lots of $\dfrac{1}{10\,000}$ is (   ).

(c) There are 10 mangos in a bag. If everyone ate 0.1 bag of mangos, then 11 people ate (   ) bag of mangos.

(d) There are 100 fruit candies in a jar. They are divided equally into 100 parts. A set of 25 fruit candies is (   ) of the whole pack. (Express the answer as a decimal.)

6.7 Understanding decimals (6)

Learning objective

Recognise and write decimal equivalents to tenths, hundredths and thousandths

Basic questions

1 Fill in the brackets.

(a) There are (   ) lots of $\frac{1}{100}$ in 0.08. There are (   ) thousandths in 0.721.

(b) A decimal number with three decimal places has the digit 2 in all the tens, tenths and hundredths places. The rest of the places are zeros. This number is (   ).

(c) A number consists of 2 hundreds, 15 ones and 95 hundredths. This number is (   ).

(d) A number consists of 1 thousand, 2 tens, 6 hundredths and 1 thousandth. This number is (   ).

(e) 803 hundredths make (   ).

(f) The place value of 8 in the far left digit of the number 8.008 is (   ) times the place value of 8 in the far right.

(g) There are (   ) 0.01s in 27.93.

(h) Four hundred point zero zero four can be written as (   ). It is a (   ) decimal number.

(i) 0.707 is read as (   ). It is a (   ) decimal number.

(j) There are (   ) decimal numbers with two decimal places that are greater than 3.9 but less than 4.0.

2 Multiple choice questions.

(a) What value does the digit '6' in each of the following numbers stand for?

7.26(   )   60.32 (   )   78.006 (   )   0.619 (   )

A. 6 tens.   B. 6 one-tenths.

C. 6 one-hundredths.   D. 6 one-thousandths.

(b) Sixty 0.01s are (   ).

A. 60   B. 6   C. 0.6   D. 0.06

(c) Five 0.1s are equivalent to (   ) 0.001s.

A. 50   B. 500   C. 5000   D. 50 000

(d) 7 tens and 7 tenths make (   ).

A. 700.70   B. 7.70   C. 70.70   D. 70.070

(e) 0.0132 is (   ) 13.2.

A. one tenth of   B. one hundredth of

C. one thousandth of   D. 1000 times

(f) A decimal with one decimal place stands for (   ).

A decimal with two decimal places stands for (   ).

A decimal with three decimal places stands for (   ).

A. thousandths   B. hundredths

C. tenths   D. ten thousandths

Challenge and extension question

3 A mixed decimal number with three decimal places has the following features: (i) The whole number part is 3 less than the greatest two-digit number. (ii) The digit in the tenths place is 6 greater than the digit in the hundredths place, and their sum is 10. (iii) The digit in the thousandths place is equal to the digit in the tens place. What is the number?

6.8 Comparing decimals (1)

 Learning objective

Compare and order decimal numbers

 Basic questions

1 Let's have a try.

(a) Locate each number below on the number line and mark a small point to indicate it.

$$5.8 \qquad 2.1 \qquad 4.5 \qquad 7.7 \qquad 0.4$$

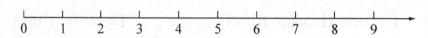

(b) Which one of the decimal numbers above is the greatest? And which one is the least?

(c) Is the value of each number related to its distances to the origin point, zero, on the number line?

(d) Put the numbers in order from the greatest to the least.

2 Fill in the brackets.

When comparing two decimals, we first compare the (　　　　) part; the greater the whole number part, the (　　) the number. If the whole number parts are the same, then we compare the digits in the (　　) place; the greater the digit in the (　　) place, the greater the decimal, and so on.

3 Use the method indicated above to fill in the ◯ with $>$ or $<$.

(a) 1.5 ◯ 1.06   (b) 0.101 ◯ 0.099   (c) 12.25 ◯ 12.26

(d) 0.519 ◯ 0.521 (e) $\frac{1}{2}$ ◯ 0.51   (f) 101.1 ◯ 99.2

4 Put the decimal numbers in order, starting with the greatest.
(a) 0.9, 0.909, 9.09, 0.99 _____

(b) 22.02, 22.20, 22.202, 22.002 _____

5 Study the table below. Who is the tallest? Who is the heaviest?

Name	John	Mathew	Joan	Imogen
Height (cm)	1.39	1.33	1.38	1.30
Weight (kg)	25.3	28.2	24	25.2

6 In a competition, three people were asked to make the same number of dolls. It took Emily 6.5 hours, Joshua 6.25 hours, and Eileen 5.9 hours to finish the task. Who worked the fastest?

 Challenge and extension questions

7 Write a suitable number in each box.

0.☐6 $<$ 0.07   9.31 $>$ 9.3☐   6.☐4 $>$ 6.54

8 Use the digits 0, 2, 4, 6 and decimal point to make pure decimal numbers with two decimal places. Put them in order from the least to the greatest.

6.9 Comparing decimals (2)

 Learning objective

Compare, order and round decimal numbers

 Basic questions

1 Compare the numbers and fill in the ◯ with > or <.

(a) 34. 1 ◯ 3. 41   (b) 0. 96 ◯ 0. 69   (c) 0. 80 ◯ 0. 801

(d) 0. 103 ◯ 103   (e) $\frac{1}{100}$ ◯ 0. 001   (f) 8. 139 ◯ 8. 130

2 Mark the following decimals on the number line and fill in the brackets.

1.9,   4.7,   5.2,   7.5,   9.8,   3.4

```
 |‖‖‖‖|‖‖‖‖|‖‖‖‖|‖‖‖‖|‖‖‖‖|‖‖‖‖|‖‖‖‖|‖‖‖‖|‖‖‖‖|‖‖‖‖|
 0    1    2    3    4    5    6    7    8    9    10
```

(a) Rounding 1.9 to the nearest whole number, the result is (   )

(b) Rounding 4.7 to the nearest whole number, the result is (   )

(c) Rounding 5.2 to the nearest whole number, the result is (   )

(d) Rounding 7.5 to the nearest whole number, the result is (   )

(e) Rounding 9.8 to the nearest whole number, the result is (   )

(f) Rounding 3.4 to the nearest whole number, the result is (   )

(g) When rounding a decimal with one decimal place to the nearest whole number, we look at the digit in the tenths place. If the digit is greater than or equal to (   ), we round it up and the result is the whole number part plus one. If the digit is less than (   ), the result is the whole number part itself.

3 Draw lines to match each decimal number in the first row with its nearest whole numbers.

| 1.6 | | 212.9 | | 1.9 | | 213.1 | | 0.3 | | 2.5 |

| 3 | 2 | 16 | 213 | 212 | 0 | 214 | 1 |

4 Put the measures in order, starting from the least.

(a) 2 m, 2.4 m, 2.04 m, 2.44 m _____

(b) 0.58 kg, 0.59 kg, 5.8 kg, 5.9 kg _____

5 Joan has £9 and 80p. Tom has £9.08. Who has more? (Hint: £1＝100p)

Challenge and extension questions

6 Round the following decimals with two decimal places to their nearest whole numbers.

11.09,   34.77,   15.25,   7.45,   111.118,   1000.41

7 The weights of four people, A, B, C and D, are 21.46 kg, 21.52 kg, 21.38 kg, and 21.5 kg. They are not in order. Person A is heavier than Person D but lighter than Person C. Person D is lighter than Person B, and Person A is heavier than Person B. What is the weight of each person?

6.10 Properties of decimals

Learning objective

Identify properties of decimals, including the value of any zeros

Basic questions

1 Can you draw three lines, which are 0.1 m, 0.10 m, and 0.100 m long respectively? What do you find? Fill in the circles and blanks.

(a) From 1 m＝100 cm, we can see 0.1 m ◯ 0.10 m ◯ 0.100 m.

(b) Properties of decimals: When zeros are added or removed at the (　　) of the decimal part of a decimal number, the value of the number remains (　　).

2 Write the following numbers into the ovals as indicated.
3.90, 10.005, 300.00, 0.103, 100, 20.002, 1.400

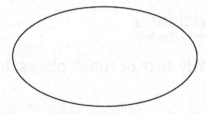

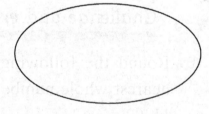

Zeros can be dropped off at the end of the decimal part from any places.　　No zeros can be dropped off.

3 Use the properties of decimals to simplify the following decimals.

(a) 600.060 ＝ (　　)　　　　(b) 3.500 ＝ (　　)

(c) 700.00 ＝ (　　)　　　　(d) 13.90 ＝ (　　)

(e) 303.330 ＝ (　　)　　　　(f) 10.100 ＝ (　　)

4 Rewrite the decimal numbers as decimals with three decimal places without changing the value of the numbers.

(a) $1.4 = ($ $)$　　　　(b) $5.04 = ($ $)$　　(c) $8 = ($ $)$

(d) $30.40000 = ($ $)$　(e) $9.4 = ($ $)$　　(f) $10 = ($ $)$

5 Compare the numbers and fill in the $\bigcirc$ with $>$, $<$ or $=$.

(a) $1.01 \bigcirc 1.10$　　(b) $3.4 \bigcirc 3.04$　　　(c) $20.2 \bigcirc 20.200$

(d) $4.73 \bigcirc 4.37$　　(e) $16 \bigcirc 16.000$　　(f) $5.06 \bigcirc 5.060$

(g) $9.89 \bigcirc 9.98$　　(h) $13.41 \bigcirc 13.410$　(i) $\frac{1}{100} \bigcirc 0.010$

(j) $7.07 \bigcirc 7.70$

6 Multiple choice questions.

(a) In the following, the decimal number equal to 26.06 is (   ).

　　A. 26.60　　　B. 2.6060　　　C. 26.060　　　D. 26.006

(b) When zeros are added or removed (   ), the value of the decimal number remains unchanged.

　　A. at the end of a number

　　B. in the middle of a number

　　C. at the end of the decimal part of a number

　　D. after the decimal point

(c) There are (   ) numbers greater than 1.1 but less than 1.2.

　　A. 0　　　　　B. 1　　　　　C. 10　　　　　D. infinite

(d) In the following numbers, the number whose value is unchanged after each '0' in it is dropped off is (   ).

　　A. 40.34　　　B. 5.910　　　C. 9.02　　　D. 700

(e) Among the following pairs of numbers, the two equal numbers are in (   ).

　　A. 57.00 and 75.00　　　　B. 8.04 and 80.4

　　C. 909.90 and 909.9　　　　D. 10.01 and 10.10

Challenge and extension questions

7 Fill in the table.

	Rewrite as a decimal with one decimal place	Rewrite as a decimal with two decimal places	Rewrite as a decimal with three decimal places
0.60		/	
37			
19.900			/

8 Put the numbers 0.112, 0.120, 1.1, 0.1021 and $\dfrac{1}{1000}$ in order from the least to the greatest.

9 A, B, C and D are four pure decimal numbers. B has three decimal places and its value is between A and C. C is 0.01 greater than A and D is 0.001 greater than B but less than C. A is 0.02. What number does C stand for? What numbers do B and D stand for?

Unit test 6

1 Fill in the brackets.

(a) When rewriting $\frac{29}{100}$ as a decimal, it is (   ). It is read as

(   ). It is a decimal with (   )

decimal places. It is a (   ) (choose 'pure' or 'mixed')

decimal. It consists of (   ) hundredths. Adding (   ) to

it makes 1.

(b) The hundreds place is the (   ) place to the left of the

decimal point. The hundredths place is the (   ) place to

the right of the decimal point.

(c) 5 tenths and 7 hundredths make (   ).

(d) 9.06 plus (   ) hundredths is 10.

(e) $0.37=($ $)\times1+($ $)\times0.1+($ $)\times0.01$

(f) 1200 thousandths is (   ). It is a (   ) (choose 'pure' or

'mixed') decimal, consisting of (   ) one(s) and (   ) tenths.

(g) In 57.067, the '7' in the whole number part is in the (   )

place and its place value is 7 (   ). The '7' in the decimal

part is in the (   ) place and its place value is 7 (   ).

(h) In 12.21, the value of the digit '1' on the left is (   ) times

the value of the digit '1' on the right. The value of '2' on

the right is (   ) times the value of '2' on the left.

(i) The whole number part in a decimal is the least two-digit

number and the decimal part is the greatest pure decimal with

two decimal places. This decimal number is (   ).

(j) Two hundred point zero two can be written in numerals as

(   ). Its decimal part has two (   ). Without

changing its value, it can be written as a decimal with three

decimal places, that is (   ).

2 Write the following fractions as decimal numbers.

(a) $\dfrac{1}{4}=$ (b) $\dfrac{1}{2}=$ (c) $\dfrac{3}{4}=$

(d) $\dfrac{1}{10}=$ (e) $\dfrac{17}{100}=$ (f) $\dfrac{999}{1000}=$

3 Write the following decimals as fractions.

(a) $0.3=$ (b) $0.25=$ (c) $0.07=$

(d) $0.21=$ (e) $0.75=$ (f) $0.191=$

4 Use the properties of decimals to complete the table. The first two have been done for you.

Decimal numbers	Can some zeros be dropped off without changing the value? (Yes or No)	If the answer is yes, write the number after dropping the zeros
0.110	Yes	0.11
0.205	No	Not applicable (or N/A)
0.7040		
7.000		
68.0100		
200.060		
0.007		
230.0900		

5 Multiple choice questions.

(a) There are (   ) thousandths in 1.2.

     A. 20   B. 200   C. 120   D. 1200

(b) There are (   ) decimal numbers with one decimal place greater than 9 but less than 10.

     A. 8   B. 9   C. 10   D. infinite

(c) In a race, it took Matthew 2.91 minutes, James 3.1 minutes, Tim 3.05 minutes and Alvin 2.90 minutes to complete the whole course. The person who gained second place was (   ).

A. Matthew   B. James   C. Tim   D. Alvin

(d) The greatest pure decimal number with two decimal places is (   ).

A. 99.99   B. 9.99   C. 0.09   D. 0.99

6 True or false.

(a) Adding or dropping any 'zeros' after the decimal point of a decimal number will not change the value of the decimal number. (   )

(b) After simplifying 0.500 by dropping the zeros at its end, it is 5. (   )

(c) After dropping the last two zeros in 200, the value remains unchanged. (   )

(d) 0.7 metres and 0.70 metres refer to the same length. (   )

(e) Rewriting 2.4 as a decimal number with three decimal places without changing the value, it is 2.004. (   )

7 Fill in the brackets with decimal numbers with two decimal places.

(a) 36 pence=(   ) pounds   (b) 4 pence=(   ) pounds

(c) 110 pounds=(   ) pounds

(d) 1 pound 60 pence=(   ) pounds

(e) 3 pounds and 4 pence=(   ) pounds

(f) 90 pence=(   ) pounds

8 Comparing decimals.

(a) Put 0.5, 0.055, 0.505 and 0.550 in order from the greatest to the least.

(   )>(   )>(   )>(   )

(b) Put the following measures in order from the shortest to the longest: 5 km 4 m, 0.0054 km, 5.04 km, 5.40 km

_____

9 Round the following decimals with one decimal place to their nearest whole numbers. Write the result in the bracket below.

15.9   0.1   10.4   119.5
(   )   (   )   (   )   (   )

10 Use the digits 0, 1, 3, 5 and decimal point to write numbers as indicated.

(a) All decimal numbers less than 1 and with three decimal places.

(b) All decimal numbers greater than 5 and with three decimal places.

(c) All decimal numbers which contain zero, but the zero is not read out, and have two decimal places.

11 In a maths test, the average score of a class is 92.35 marks. Tim's score is 2.5 marks higher than the average. Lynn's score is 0.7 marks lower than the average. James' score is 3.4 marks higher than the average, and Mary's score is 0.5 marks lower than the average. Among the four, who has the highest score?

Chapter 7   Statistics (Ⅲ)

7.1   Knowing line graphs (1)

 Learning objective

Interpret information presented in line graphs and time graphs

 Basic questions

1 One day, Jo was ill and in hospital. The line graph below shows her body temperatures recorded by the nurse at different times of the day (graphs like this are also called time graphs).
Read the graph and answer the questions below.

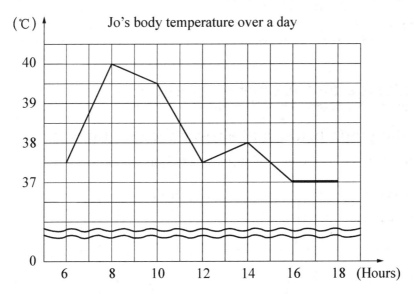

(a) What does the horizontal axis represent?
What does the vertical axis represent?
What does a single unit on the vertical axis stand for (in Celsius)?

(b) At what time did Jo have the highest body temperature? What was her temperature at that time?

(c) The nurse checked Jo's temperature every _____ hours.

(d) When did Jo's temperature go up the fastest?

(e) When did her temperature go down the fastest?

(f) When was there no change in her temperature?

(g) Did Jo get better or worse? How can you tell?

2 Use the information given in the line graph above to complete the table below.

Time	06:00	08:00	10:00	12:00	14:00	16:00	18:00
Temperature (℃)							

Challenge and extension question

3 Read the graph below and answer the questions.

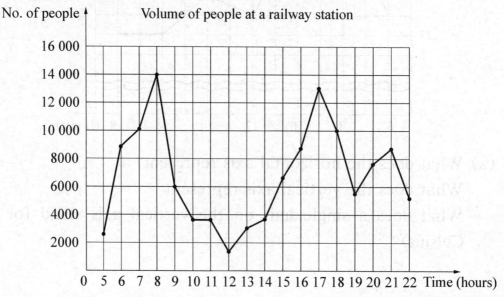

(a) At what times did the volume of people reach a peak at the station? Why did it reach a peak at those times?

(b) At what time was the volume of people the least at the station? Why do you think this is?

(c) What other questions can you pose? Discuss the questions with your friends.

7.2　Knowing line graphs (2)

Learning objective

Interpret information presented in line graphs and bar charts

Basic question

1 The line graphs below show the sales of wool quilts and picnic blankets in a shop in 2014. Read the graphs carefully and answer the questions below.

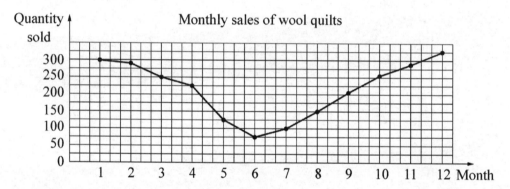

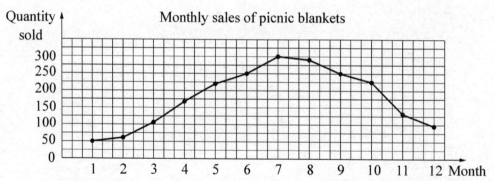

(a) In each graph, what does the horizontal axis represent? What does the vertical axis represent?

(b) Which month has the highest sales volume of the wool quilts? Which month has the lowest? What is the difference of the sales volume between these two months? What is the sum?

(c) From which month to which month does the sales volume of wool quilts show an upward tendency? From which month to which month does it show a downward tendency?

(d) Which month has the highest sales volume of picnic blankets? Which month has the lowest? What is the difference of the sales volume between these two months? What is the sum?

(e) From which month to which month does the sales volume of picnic blankets show an upward tendency? From which month to which month does it show a downward tendency?

(f) If the above two line graphs showed the monthly sales of picnic blankets and wool quilts but without the titles, could you use your knowledge from daily life to tell which one is a sales graph for picnic blankets and which one is for wool quilts? Give your reasons.

Challenge and extension question

2 Two statistical graphs are shown below. Observe the graphs carefully and answer the questions.

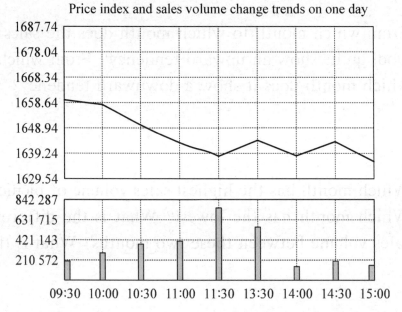

Price index and sales volume change trends on one day

(a) The top graph is a (   ) graph and the bottom graph is a (   ) chart.

(b) Choose the correct answer below and write it in the brackets.
A bar chart shows the change of the data by (   ), and a line graph shows the change of the data by (   ).
A. the upward or downward trend of the line
B. the thicknesses of the bars
C. the heights of the bars   D. the length of the line

(c) Given that the top graph shows the price index and the bottom graph shows the sales volume, the highest point of the price index was found at (   ), and the change of the index showed a (   ) trend.

(d) The highest sales volume was at (   ) and the lowest was at (   ). The sales volume from (   ) to (   ) showed an upward trend.

7.3 Knowing line graphs (3)

Learning objective

Interpret information presented in line graphs

Basic questions

1. Think carefully and then fill in the brackets with the suitable answers given below.

   A. line   B. trend   C. change   D. magnitude

   (a) A line graph can show clearly not only the (   ) of the quantity, but also the (   ) of the quantity.

   (b) A line graph is often used to show a (   ) over a period of time.

   (c) It is often more appropriate to present statistical data such as monthly sales in a year, which emphasises the change of the data over a period of time, by using a (   ) graph.

2. Read the graph and answer the questions from (a) to (h).

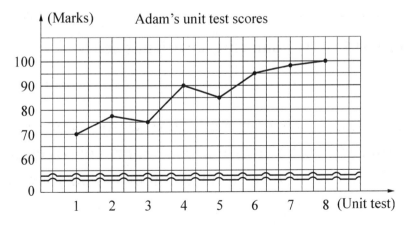

   (a) What are Adam's highest and lowest scores, respectively?

(b) What does the ～～～～ part of the graph mean?

(c) From which unit test onwards did the test scores go upward steadily?

(d) Which unit test score shows the greatest improvement?

(e) Did Adam's score mostly improve or decline in these unit tests?

Challenge and extension questions

(f) Fill in the table based on the line graph above and work out the answers.

Unit	One	Two	Three	Four	Five	Six	Seven	Eight
Scores		77					98	

(g) Can you briefly comment on Adam's study?

(h) Can you use your own maths test scores over a recent period of time to make a table, and then construct a statistical graph? Please also try to give comments on your own study.

7.4 Constructing line graphs

Learning objective

Construct line graphs and interpret information from them

Basic questions

1. Steps for constructing a line graph.
   (a) Decide the scope and structure of the line graph.
   (b) Decide the content of the graph, such as the title and (   ) etc.
   (c) Draw and mark the scale points on the (   ), so that the maximum scale points on both the horizontal axis and the vertical axis can show the time (order) and the greatest value of the data.

2. The table below shows the number of pedestrians crossing at a busy road intersection recorded by a traffic warden in a week. Construct a line graph using the data and work out the answers.

Time	Monday	Tuesday	Wednesday	Thursday	Friday	Saturday	Sunday
Number of people	40	44	46	38	30	28	18

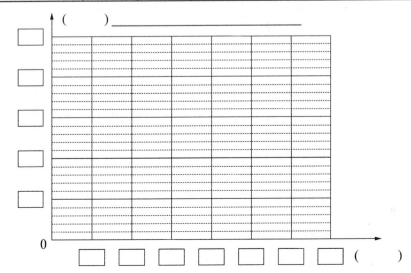

(a) Which day had the most pedestrians crossing in the week? What was the number of pedestrians crossing?

(b) Between which two days was there the greatest decrease in the number of pedestrians crossing the intersection?

(c) From the statistics of that week, what is the tendency of people crossing the intersection?

(d) What is the total number of pedestrians crossing recorded over the whole week?

3 Can you use the information presented in the table in the above question to make a bar chart?
(a) Please show your results below.

(   )

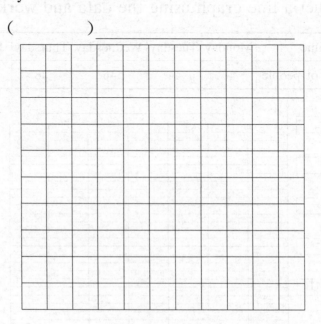

(b) Which graphical method, a line graph or a bar chart, do you think is more appropriate to present the data of pedestrians crossing as reported in the above question? Briefly give your reason.

Challenge and extension question

4 Use your heights from the age of 6 to the present to complete the table below. Then construct a line graph and predict your height after 3 more years.

Age						
Height(cm)						

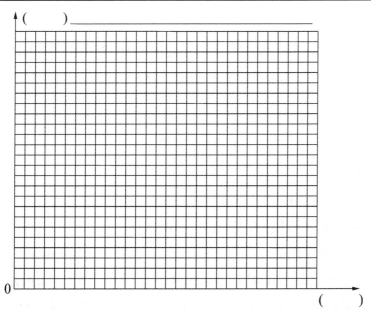

My prediction:

Unit test 7

1 Work these out mentally, and then write the answers.

$50 \times 10 =$ $360 \div 90 =$ $600 \div 30 + 30 =$ $8 \times 300 =$

$206 - 16 =$ $40 \times 7 + 70 =$ $60 \div 5 \div 12 =$ $540 \div 9 =$

2 Use the column method to calculate. (Check the answers to the questions marked with $*$.)

(a) $98 \times 42 =$ (b) $24 \times 302 =$ (c) $* 789 \times 4 =$

(d) $450 \div 50 =$ (e) $1320 \div 60 =$ (f) $* 7843 \div 70 =$

3 Work these out step by step. (Calculate smartly if possible.)

$116 \div 4 + 884$ $786 + 659 + 114$ $250 \times 17 \times 4$

4 Fill in the brackets.

(a) Choose from the following words:

     A. straight lines   B. change of the quantity

     C. magnitude of the quantity   D. unit length

In a line graph, a (   ) on the vertical axis represents a certain quantity of data. Based on the (   ), each point is marked accordingly and then all the points are connected with (   ) from left to right based on the horizontal axis. The line graph shows the (   ) through the ups and downs of the line.

(b) The graph on the right shows the numbers of award winners in maths competitions of different grade levels in a school.

Numbers of award winners in maths competitions in different year groups

(i) There are (   ) winners in Year 1 and (   ) winners in Year 4 in the competitions.

(ii) Among the five year groups, Year (   ) has the most award winners.

(iii) The number of award winners in Year 3 is (   ) times that of Year 1.

(iv) The difference in the number of winners between Year (   ) and Year (   ) is the greatest.

(v) The total number of winners in all the five grade levels is (   ).

❺ Multiple choice questions.

(a) A line graph is suitable to present statistical data which change over (   ).

A. the magnitude of quantity

B. time or sequence

C. types of statistics

(b) The graph below which shows the tendency of the greatest increase is (   ).

A.   B.   C.   D.   E.

6 Read the graph below and answer the questions.

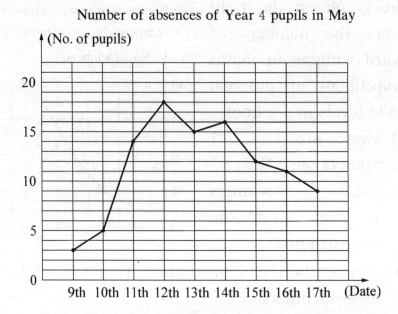

Number of absences of Year 4 pupils in May

(a) Which day had the greatest number of Year 4 pupils on absence since 9 May? How many pupils were absent?

(b) Between which two days was there a sudden increase in the number of absentees?

(c) On which days did the number of absentees decrease?

(d) What do you predict to be the number of absentees on 18 May?

(e) What is the total number of absences of Year 4 pupils during this period?

7 In a campaign for children in developing countries, the number of books donated by a primary school from Year 1 to Year 5 is as follows: 50 books from Year 1, 65 books from Year 2, 85 books from Year 3, 150 books from Year 4 and 230 books from Year 5.

(a) Use the information given to complete the table below.

Year group	Year 1	Year 2	Year 3	Year 4	Year 5
Number of books donated					

(b) Construct a line graph based on the data given.

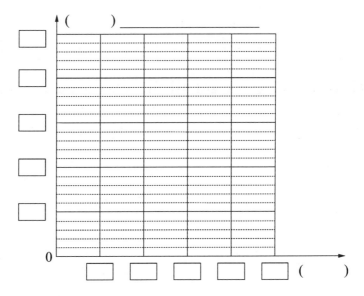

(c) What tendency did it reveal about the relationship between the number of books donated and the different levels of year groups?

(d) Construct a bar chart based on the data given.

( )_____

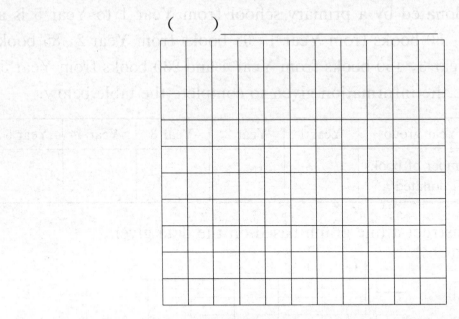

(e) How many books did all the year groups donate in total?

Chapter 8 Geometry and measurement (Ⅰ)

8.1 Acute and obtuse angles

 Learning objective

Identify acute and obtuse angles

 Basic questions

1 Is each angle marked below in the diagram an acute angle, right angle, or obtuse angle? Write your answer in the blank.

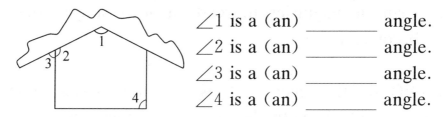

∠1 is a (an) _____ angle.

∠2 is a (an) _____ angle.

∠3 is a (an) _____ angle.

∠4 is a (an) _____ angle.

2 On a clock face the hour hand and the minute hand form an angle. What angles do they form at different times? Write the times in the correct boxes below.

3 o'clock,   half past 3,   4 o'clock,   half past 5,

9 o'clock,   half past 9,   11 o'clock

Acute angles	Right angles	Obtuse angles

3 Count and find out the number of right angles in each digit below. Fill in the brackets.

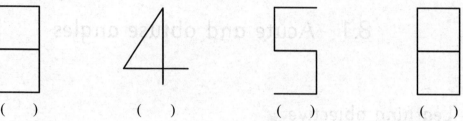

( )　　　　　　( )　　　　　　( )　　　　　　( )

4 True or false.

(a) The angles smaller than an obtuse angle are right angles.

( )

(b) All the acute angles are smaller than a right angle. ( )

(c) When half past 9 shows on the clock face, the hour hand and the minute hand form a right angle. ( )

(d) Using a magnifier to read an acute angle, the angle will become greater. ( )

5 Identify whether each angle is an acute, obtuse or right angle. Fill in the blanks with the numbers of these shapes. (Note: you may use a set square to help.)

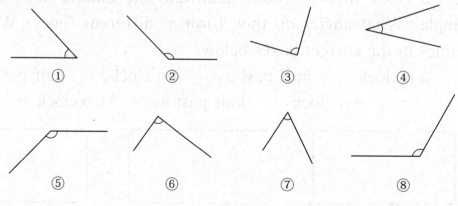

Acute angles: _____　　　Right angles: _____
Obtuse angles: _____

Challenge and extension questions

6 Count the numbers of faces and angles on the three-dimensional figure below. How many faces are there? How many angles are there?

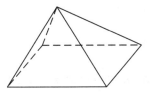

7 Draw four right angles with two lines.

8.2 Triangles and quadrilaterals (1)

Learning objective

Understand the properties of triangles and quadrilaterals

Basic questions

1 Which shapes below are triangles and which are quadrilaterals? Fill in the blanks with the numbers of these shapes.

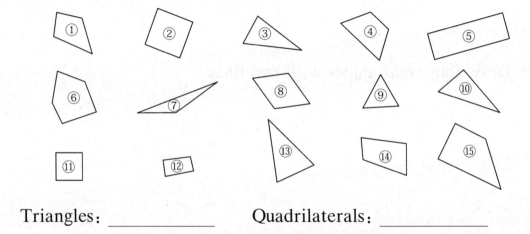

Triangles: _____   Quadrilaterals: _____

2 Look at each figure below and draw the same figure on the right-hand side of the grid.

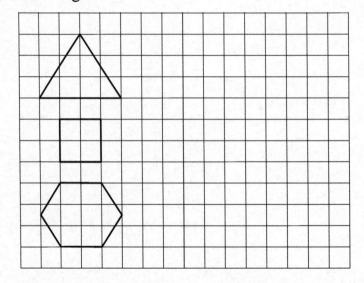

3 Fill in the brackets.

(a) A triangle can be formed using (　　) sticks. Four sticks of the same size are needed to form a (　　　　　).

(b) A triangle has (　　) sides and (　　) angles. A quadrilateral has (　　) sides and (　　) angles.

(c) Both rectangles and squares are (　　　　　). The (　　) sides of a rectangle are equal. A square has (　　) equal sides.

(d) A (　　) is a special rectangle.

(e) Make a count. In the figure on the right, there are (　　) triangles and (　　) quadrilaterals.

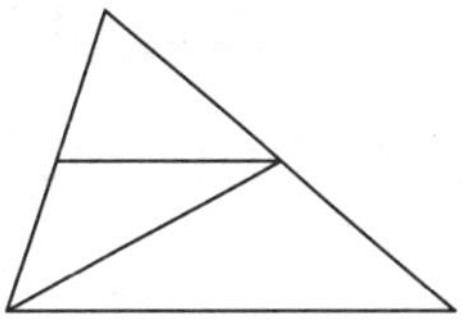

4 True or false.

(a) A diagram with four lines is a quadrilateral. (　　)

(b) A rectangle is a special square. (　　)

(c) A quadrilateral with four right angles is a rectangle. (　　)

(d) A triangle is a special quadrilateral. (　　)

5 Draw a line in each figure to divide it into two shapes as indicated.

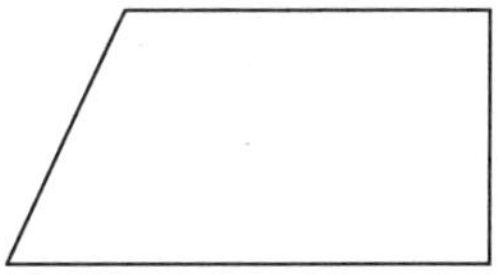

(a) two quadrilaterals 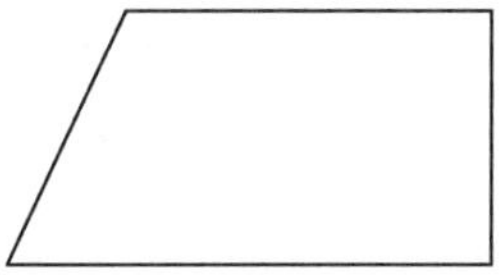　　(b) two triangles 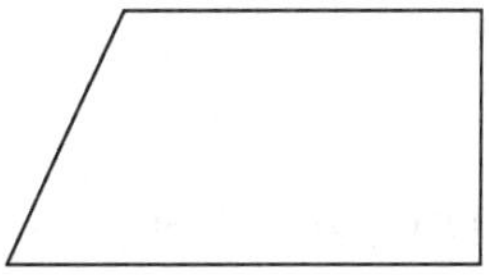　　(c) a triangle and a quadrilateral

Challenge and extension question

6 Count the figures and then fill in the brackets.

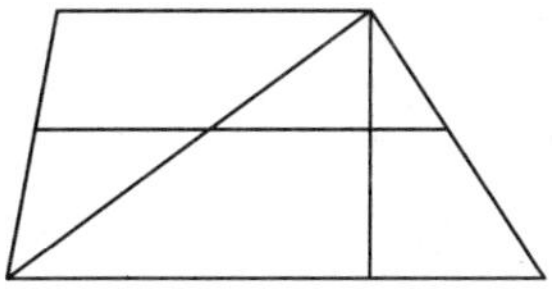

There are (　　) triangles.
There are (　　) quadrilaterals.

8.3 Triangles and quadrilaterals (2)

 Learning objective

Understand the properties of triangles and quadrilaterals

 Basic questions

1 Write the name of each figure below.

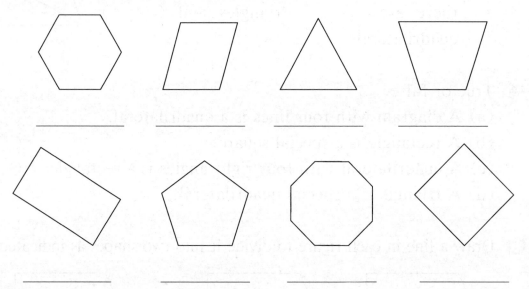

_____   _____   _____   _____

_____   _____   _____   _____

2 True or false.

(a) Both squares and rectangles are special quadrilaterals. (　　)

(b) A figure with three sides and three angles is a triangle.

(　　)

(c) A quadrilateral with four right angles is a square.　　(　　)

(d) A figure formed by five connected lines is a pentagon.

(　　)

3 Sheltering baby animals.

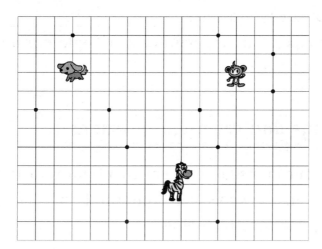

(a) Connect the dots to form the shelter for each baby animal.

(b) The shape of the shelter for the puppy is a (   ). The
shape of the shelter for the baby monkey is a (   ).
The shape of the shelter for the baby zebra is a (   ).

(c) The shelter for the (   ) is the largest.

4 Look at each shape below and then fill in the blanks. You may
use a set square or ruler to measure.

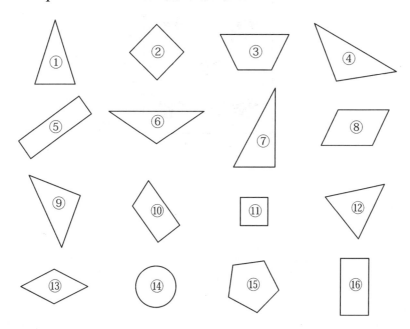

(a) The shapes with one or more right angles are _____.

(b) The quadrilaterals are _____.

(c) The shapes that are neither a triangle nor a quadrilateral are

_____.

Challenge and extension questions

⑤ Make one cut in a square to get two figures of the same shape and size. How many ways can you think of? Draw to show your methods in the squares below.

⑥ In the figure shown below, there are 5 chicks in a square cage. Draw another square in this square cage so that all 5 chicks are separated.

8.4 Classification of triangles (1)

 Learning objective

Classify triangles

Basic questions

1 Observe the features of the triangles below. Classify these triangles by their features.

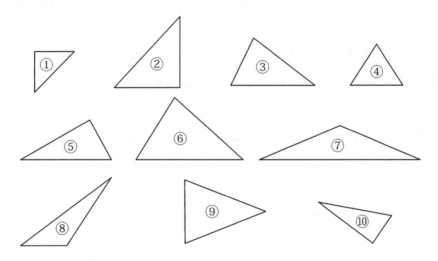

(a) A triangle with one right angle is called a (   ).
    They are ①, _____ , _____ and _____ .
(b) A triangle with an (   ) is called an obtuse-angled
    triangle. They are _____ and _____ .
(c) A triangle with all three angles being (   ) is called an
    acute-angled triangle. They are _____ .

2 Look at the triangles on the next page. What types of triangles are
they? Fill in the brackets. (Choose from acute-angled, right-angled
or obtuse-angled.)

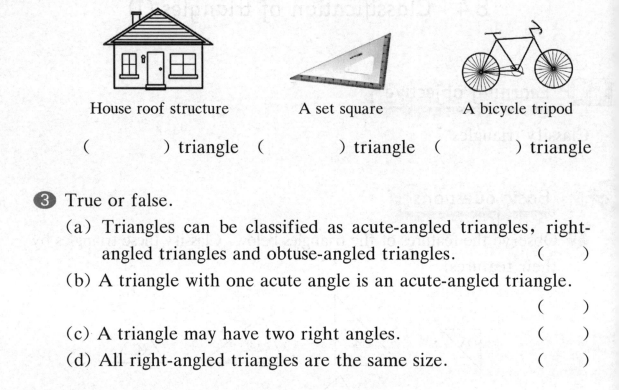

House roof structure   A set square   A bicycle tripod

（　　　　）triangle　（　　　　）triangle　（　　　　）triangle

3 True or false.

(a) Triangles can be classified as acute-angled triangles，right-angled triangles and obtuse-angled triangles.   （　　）

(b) A triangle with one acute angle is an acute-angled triangle.

    （　　）

(c) A triangle may have two right angles.   （　　）

(d) All right-angled triangles are the same size.   （　　）

4 Draw an acute-angled triangle，a right-angled triangle and an obtuse-angled triangle on the grid below.

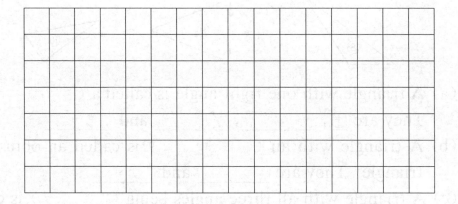

5 Divide the figures.

(a) Draw a line to divide the following quadrilateral into two acute-angled triangles.

(b) Draw a line to divide the following quadrilateral into two obtuse-angled triangles.

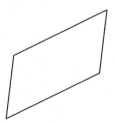

Challenge and extension question

6　In the figure below there are five angles in a pentagon. If one of the five corners is cut off, how many angles are there in the remaining part of the figure?

8.5 Classification of triangles (2)

 Learning objective

Classify triangles

 Basic questions

1 Classify the triangles as indicated. Fill in the blanks.

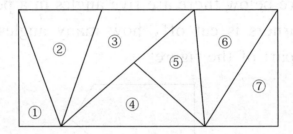

The acute-angled triangles are _____. The right-angled triangles are _____. The obtuse-angled triangles are _____.

2 Multiple choice questions.

(a) A triangle has at least (   ) acute angles.

　A. 1　　　　　　　　　　　B. 2

　C. 3　　　　　　　　　　　D. cannot be determined

(b) In a triangle, if the greatest angle is an acute angle, it is (   ) triangle.

　A. a right-angled　　　　　B. an acute-angled

　C. an obtuse-angled　　　　D. cannot be determined

(c) Two right-angled triangles of the same size and shape can be combined into (   ).

　A. a right-angled triangle　　B. an acute-angled triangle

　C. an obtuse-angled triangle

　D. all of the above are possible

(d) The part of the figure covered by the paper as shown in the diagram on the right is (   ).

    A. a right-angled triangle

    B. a rectangle

    C. a square

    D. all of the above are possible

(e) In the following shapes, (   ) does not have any acute angles.

    A. an acute-angled triangle   B. a rectangle

    C. a right-angled triangle   D. an obtuse-angled triangle

(f) Fold a piece of paper in half from top to bottom and then fold it again in half from left to right. Now unfold the paper, there are (   ) right angles made by the two creases.

    A. 1   B. 2   C. 3   D. 4

❸ Count the triangles in the diagram shown. There are (   ) triangles in total. There are (   ) acute-angled triangles, (   ) right-angled triangles and (   ) obtuse-angled triangles in it.

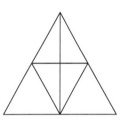

❹ Divide a triangle.

(a) Draw a line in the figure ① to divide it into an acute-angled triangle and an obtuse-angled triangle.

(b) Draw a line in the figure ② to divide it into two right-angled triangles.

(c) Draw a line in the figure ③ to divide it into one triangle and one quadrilateral.

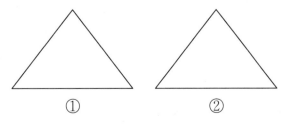

①   ②   ③

Challenge and extension question

❺ Use diagonals to divide a hexagon into four separate triangles which do not overlap. How many different ways can you find? (Rotating or flipping the hexagon does not count.) Please try it out on your own.

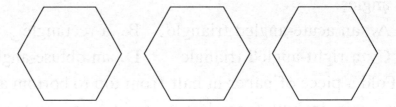

8.6　Line symmetry

Identify line symmetry in shapes and complete symmetrical figures

 Basic questions

1. Which of the following shapes have line symmetry? Put a √ or a
   × in the brackets.

(　)　　　(　)　　(　)　　(　)　　(　)

2. In each shape above, please draw a line of symmetry if it has line
   symmetry.

3. Which of the ten digits from 0 to 9 have line symmetry? Please
   write them down and draw their lines of symmetry.

4. In each grid below, half of the shape is given. Draw the other
   half so it has line symmetry.

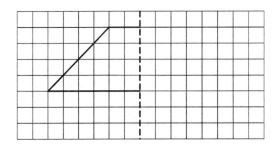 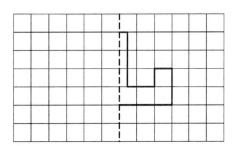

Challenge and extension questions

5 In the 26 English capital letters, how many of them have line symmetry? Please write down those letters and draw their lines of symmetry.

6 In each grid below, half of the shape is given. Draw the other half so it has line symmetry.

(a)

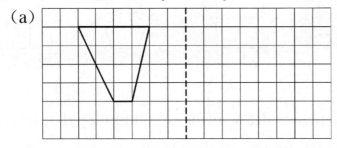

(b)

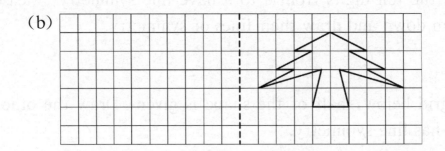

8.7 Classification of triangles (3)

Learning objective

Name and classify triangles

Basic questions

1. Fill in the brackets.
   (a) A triangle with two equal sides is called an (   ) triangle.
   (b) A triangle with three equal sides is called an (   ) triangle.
   (c) An isosceles triangle has line (   ). It has (   ) line(s) of symmetry.
   (d) An equilateral triangle has line (   ). It has (   ) line(s) of symmetry.
   (e) An equilateral triangle is a (   ) isosceles triangle.
   (f) When classified according to its angles, an equilateral triangle is an (   ) triangle.

2. Look at the triangles below and fill in the brackets with the numbers of the triangles.

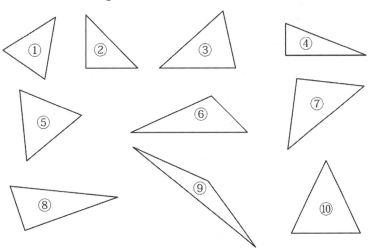

(a) The acute-angled triangles are (   ).

(b) The right-angled triangles are (   ).

(c) The obtuse-angled triangles are (   ).

(d) The isosceles triangles are (   ).

(e) The equilateral triangle is (   ).

3 Draw an isosceles triangle and an equilateral triangle and their lines of symmetry on the grid below.

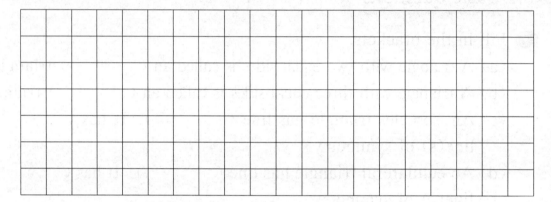

 Challenge and extension questions

4 (a) Divide an equilateral triangle into three triangles of the same shape and same size.

(b) Divide an equilateral triangle into four triangles of the same shape and same size.

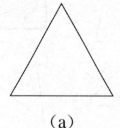

(a)

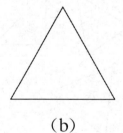

(b)

5 Fill in the brackets.

(a) In the figure below, there are (   ) isosceles triangles, of which there are (   ) equilateral triangles.

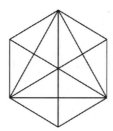

(b) In the figure below, there are (   ) isosceles triangles.

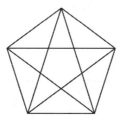

8.8 Areas

Learning objective

Find the area of shapes by counting squares

Basic questions

1. How large is each of the following figures in the grid? Express your answer using the number of the small squares it occupies and fill in the bracket.

(   ) squares   (   ) squares   (   ) squares   (   ) squares

2. The figure below shows the floor plan of Tom's new house.

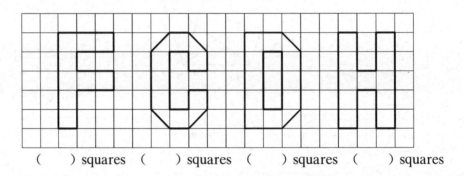

166

Answer the following questions based on the floor plan:

The master bedroom occupies (   ) squares.

The bedroom occupies (   ) squares.

The lounge occupies (   ) squares.

The dining room occupies (   ) squares.

The kitchen occupies (   ) squares.

The bathroom occupies (   ) squares.

The storage room occupies (   ) squares.

The house occupies (   ) squares in total.

3 Count the number of small squares each figure occupies in the diagram and fill in the brackets.

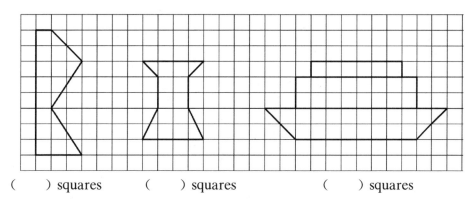

(   ) squares   (   ) squares   (   ) squares

Challenge and extension questions

4 Draw three 2-D shapes that occupy 7 squares, 9 squares and 12 squares respectively on the grid below.

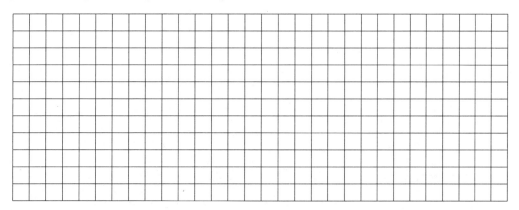

❺ Count and then write the number of squares that each figure occupies in the following grids.

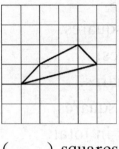   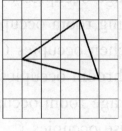

(   ) squares   (   ) squares

8.9 Areas of rectangles and squares (1)

Learning objective

Calculate the areas of squares and rectangles

Basic questions

1 The area of each small square in the figures below is 1 square centimetre, or 1 cm². Count the number of the small squares and find how many square centimetres the area of each figure is.

(a)

      (   )

Your calculation: (   )

The area of the square=

(   )

(b)

      (   )

Your calculation: (   )

The area of the rectangle=

(   )

2 Calculate the areas of the following figures.

(a)

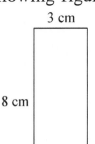

4 cm

6 cm

(b)

3 cm

8 cm

(c)

5 cm

5 cm

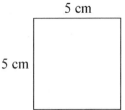

3 The length of a rectangle is 45 cm. It is 5 times the width. How many square centimetres is its area?

4 The length of a rectangle is 40 cm. It is 10 cm longer than the width. How many square centimetres is its area?

5 The length of a rectangular swimming pool is 50 m and the width is 2500 cm. What is the area of the swimming pool?

Challenge and extension questions

6 Put 12 small squares of 1 cm^2 together to form a rectangle. How many different rectangles can be formed? Draw them on the square grid below to show your answer.

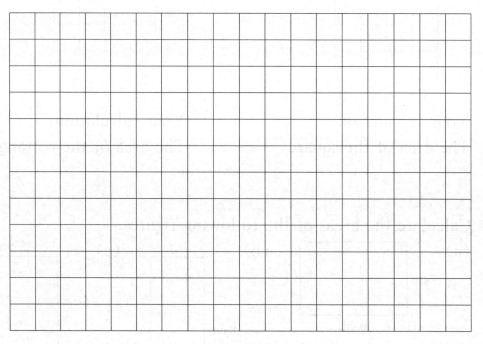

7 James cut out a square with maximum area from a rectangular piece of colour paper which is 17 cm long and 12 cm wide. How many square centimetres is the area of the square paper?

8.10 Areas of rectangles and squares (2)

 Learning objective

Calculate the areas of squares and rectangles

 Basic questions

1 Calculate the areas or the length of the figures below.

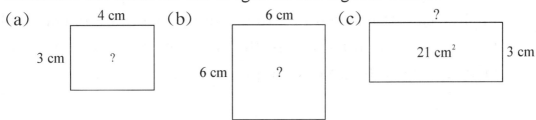

(a) 4 cm / 3 cm / ?

(b) 6 cm / 6 cm / ?

(c) ? / 21 cm^2 / 3 cm

2 The width of a rectangular table is measured as 90 cm. It is 15 cm shorter than the length. How many square centimetres is the area of the rectangular table?

3 The length of a rectangle is 18 cm. If the length is increased by 5 cm while the width is kept unchanged, the area is increased by 40 cm^2. Find the area of the original rectangle. (Hint: draw a diagram to help.)

4 Mary's father made a photo frame for her. The length of the frame is 16 cm, and the width is 22 cm. The width of the inner wooden frame is 3 cm. Find the area of the glass within the wooden frame.

5 A rectangular piece of iron sheet is 60 cm long and 50 cm wide. Mr Lee cut off its length by 15 cm and its width by 10 cm. By how many square centimetres is the area of iron sheet decreased? (Hint: draw a diagram to help.)

Challenge and extension question

6 Find the sum of all the areas of the rectangles in the figure. (unit: cm)

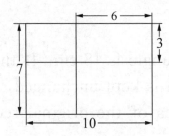

8.11 Square metres

Learning objective

Calculate the areas of squares and rectangles using square metres

Basic questions

1. Fill in the brackets.

    The area of a square with sides of length 1 m is (   ),
    written as (   ).

    The area of a square with sides of length 1 cm is (   ),
    written as (   ).

2. Fill in the brackets with suitable units.

    The area of a square table in Joan's home is about 1 (   ).

    The area of a stamp is about 12 (   ).

    The area of a classroom is about 48 (   ).

    The area of a pencil box is about 86 (   ).

    The length of the running track in the school sports field is about
    200 (   ).

    The area of the little finger nail is about 1 (   ).

    The area of Timothy's new house is about 132 (   ).

    The area of a whiteboard in a classroom is about 3 (   ).

3. Calculate the areas or the length of the following figures.

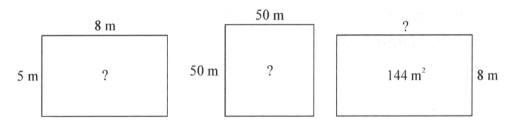

4 Mr. Jones's fishpond is 60 m long and 40 m wide. What is the area of the fishpond?

5 Joan bought a square mouse pad. Its side length is 20 cm. What is its area?

6 The length of a wheat field is 100 metres, which is four times the width. If 2 kilograms of wheat can be harvested from 1 square metre of the land, how many kilograms of wheat can be harvested from this piece of wheat field?

Challenge and extension questions

7 The side of a square flowerbed is 20 m long. Its four sides were surrounded with 2 m width of grass. Find the area of the grass.

8 The length of the straight running track in a school sports field is 80 m, and the width of the track is evenly divided into five lanes, each of which is 80 cm wide. What is the total area of the two straight running tracks?

Unit test 8

1 Look at the angles and fill in the blanks below. (Note: You may use a set square to measure.)

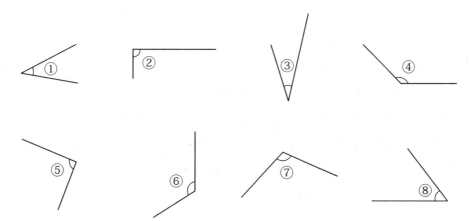

(a) The right angles are _____.

(b) The angles smaller than a right angle are called _____.
They are _____.

(c) The angles greater than a right angle are called _____.
They are _____.

2 Think carefully and classify the following figures. Write your answers in the blanks.

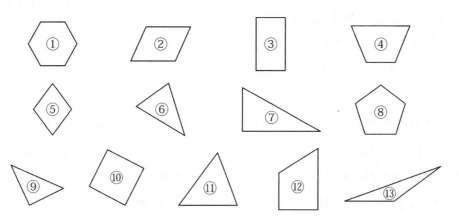

(a) The triangles are _____ . The acute-angled triangle(s) is/
are _____ . The right-angled triangle(s) is/are _____ .
The obtuse-angled triangle(s) is/are _____ .

(b) The quadrilateral(s) is/are _____ . The rectangle(s) is/are
_____ . The square(s) is/are _____ .

(c) The figures that are neither triangles nor quadrilaterals are
_____ .

3 In the following statements, there is/are (   ) correct statement(s).

(a) A square is a special rectangle.

(b) All triangles have at least two acute angles.

(c) The longer the two sides of an angle, the greater the angle.

(d) A quadrilateral with four sides of the same length is a square.

    A. 1   B. 2   C. 3   D. 4

4 In the diagram, there are (   ) triangles
and (   ) quadrilaterals in total.

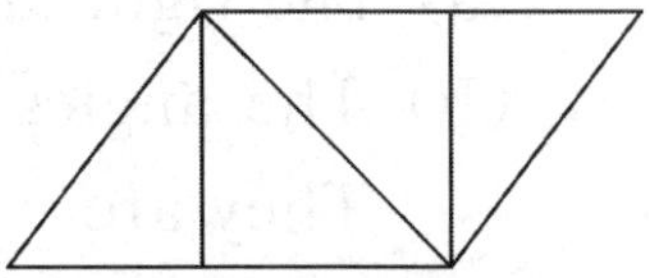

    A. 2   B. 3

    C. 4   D. 6

5 In the diagram, the figure covered by the shaded
area is (   ).

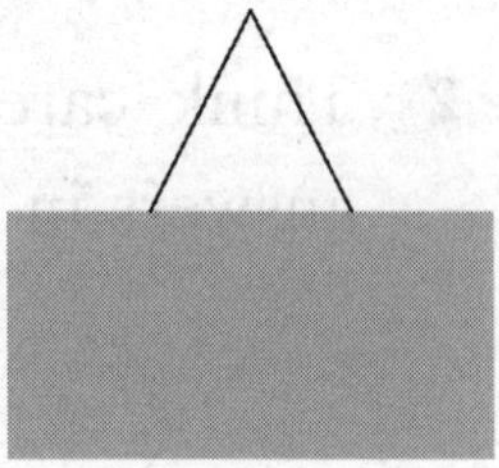

A. an acute-angled triangle

B. a right-angled triangle

C. an obtuse-angled triangle

D. all of the above are possible

6 A rectangle figure is shown below. Can you make two cuts (along
a straight line) to obtain an acute-angled triangle, an obtuse-
angled triangle and a right-angled triangle? Please draw the lines
of cutting in the figure to show your answer.

7 Fill in the brackets.

(a) The area of a square with the side length of (   ) is 1 square metre. 1 square metre is also written as (   ).

(b) Write a suitable unit in the brackets.

The height of a new born baby is about 50 (   ).

The area of a classroom is about 56 (   ).

(c) The width of a rectangle is 6 cm, and its length is 1 m. Its area is (   ).

(d) A triangle with three equal sides is called an (   ).

(e) A square has (   ) lines of symmetry. A rectangle has (   ) lines of symmetry.

8 Look at the picture and fill in the brackets with the correct letters.

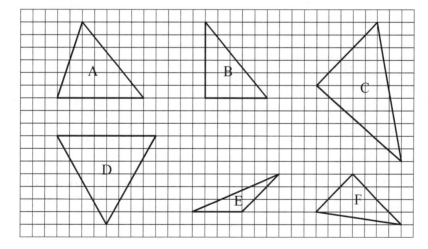

(a) The acute-angled triangle(s) is/are (   ).

(b) The obtuse-angled triangle(s) is/are (   ).

(c) The isosceles triangle(s) is/are (   ).

(d) The right-angled triangle(s) is/are (   ).

9 True or false.

(a) An equilateral triangle is also an isosceles triangle.　（　）

(b) 60 square metres is greater than 55 metres.　（　）

(c) The length of a rectangle is 4 cm and the width is 3 cm. The area is 12 cm.　（　）

10 Multiple choice questions.

(a) A triangle has two acute angles. It is a/an （　）.

　A. right-angled triangle　　　B. obtuse-angled triangle

　C. acute-angled triangle　　　D. all of the above are possible

(b) The area of a square is 100 square centimetres. The side length is （　） cm.

　A. 100　　　B. 10　　　C. 50　　　D. 25

(c) An isosceles triangle has （　） lines of symmetry.

　A. 0　　　B. 1　　　C. 2　　　D. 3

11 Find the areas of the following figures.

(a)

10 m

18 m

(b)

9 m

9 m

12 Use a set square to measure the figures and tell what figures they are, and then draw the lines of symmetry.

⓭ Find the areas of the shaded parts in the figures below by counting the squares. (The side length of each small square is 1 cm.)

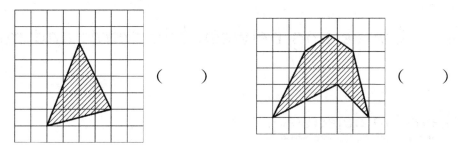

(   )   (   )

14 Application problems

(a) The width of a rectangular piece of paper is 60 cm. This is 9 cm shorter than the length. What is the area of the rectangle?

(b) The area of a floor tile is 400 cm². A room needs 750 such floor tiles to cover its total area. What is the area of the room?

(c) The length of a rectangular piece of paper is 80 cm and the width is 60 cm. After cutting out a square with maximum area from the paper, what is the area of paper that is cut off?

(d) In the diagram there is a square garden in the centre. Surrounding the garden is a gravel path 6 m wide. The area of the gravel path is 528 m². Find the area of the garden in the centre.

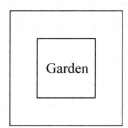

Garden

Chapter 9   Geometry and measurement (Ⅱ)

9.1   Converting between kilometres and metres

 Learning objective

Convert between units of measure

 Basic questions

① Fill in the brackets with suitable numbers.

(a) 8 km = (   )m　　　　　　(b) 1. 6 km = (   )m

(c) $\frac{1}{10}$ km = (   )m　　　　(d) 700 m = (   )km

(e) 4000 m = (   )km　　　　(f) 470 000 m = (   )km

(g) 5 km + $\frac{1}{4}$ km = (   )m　　(h) 4 km and 26 m = (   )m

(i) 19 km − 10 000 m = (   )km　(j) 1 km + 780 m = (   )m

(k) 30 km − 14 000 m = (   )m　(l) 6 km + (   )m = 6. 5 km

② Write a suitable unit in each bracket.

(a) A car can travel 110 (   ) in one hour.

(b) James can walk 70 (   ) in one minute.

(c) An aeroplane can fly about 800 (   ) in one hour.

(d) The length of the running track in a sports field is 200 (   ).

(e) The distance between London and Edinburgh is about 600 (   ).

③ Fill in the (   ) with >, < or =.

(a) 8 km (   ) 7900 m　　　(b) 3700 m (   ) 4 km

(c) 670 m (   ) 6 km　　　　(d) 10 km (   ) 10 000 m

(e) 28 km (　　) 2800 m   (f) 1 km and 60 m (　　) 160 m

(g) 8900 m (　　) 9 km   (h) 5090 m (　　) 5 km and 100 m

4 Put the following in order from the greatest to the least with >.

(a) 5 km, 4545 m, 5454 m, 4 km

_____

(b) 9 km, 20 202 m, 20 220 m, 10 000 m

_____

5 Application problems.

(a) Jonathan walked from home to school and from school to the library. How many metres did he walk in total?

Jonathan's home $\xrightarrow[1800\ m]{}$ school $\xrightarrow[1200\ m]{}$ library

(b) The total length of the Humber Bridge in East Yorkshire is 2220 m. The total length of the Forth Road Bridge in Edinburgh is 2512 m. The total length of the Severn Bridge connecting England and Wales is 1600 m. How many metres longer is the Forth Road Bridge than the Humber Bridge? What is the total length of the three bridges?

Challenge and extension question

6 (a) An aeroplane travelled 420 km in half an hour. How many metres did it travel per minute on average? How many metres did it travel per second on average?

(b) James's brother cycles to school. If he cycles 5 metres per second, how many kilometres per hour does he cycle?

9.2 Perimeters of rectangles and squares (1)

Learning objective

Calculate the perimeter of rectangles and squares

Basic questions

1 Calculate the perimeters of the following figures. (Drawing not to scale.)

(a) A square with side length of 10 cm

(b) A rectangle with length 7 cm and width 4 cm

10 cm

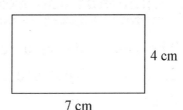

4 cm

7 cm

2 Fill in the tables.

(a) Write the perimeters and areas of the rectangles in the table.

Length	Width	Perimeter	Area
30 cm	7 cm		
40 cm	50 cm		
1 m	600 cm		

(b) Write the side length, perimeter and areas of the squares in the table.

Side length	Perimeter	Area
15 cm		
	48 m	

3 A rectangular vegetable patch is 40 m long and 5 m wide. Find the perimeter and area of the vegetable patch.

4 The perimeter of a rectangular sports field is 300 m. Given that the width is 50 m, find the length of the sports field.

5 Ben measured the swimming pool in paces. He walked the length of the pool in 100 paces and the width in 50 paces. Given that the length of Ben's pace is 50 cm, find the perimeter of the swimming pool.

Challenge and extension questions

6 The figure shows a rectangle with area of 2200 cm². What are the areas of rectangle A and rectangle B?

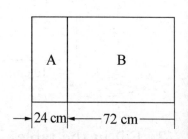

7 A 24-centimetre-long wire is bent to form a rectangle. If the length and width of the rectangle are in whole centimetres, how many different rectangles can be formed? Write down the length and width of each possible rectangle. Do all the rectangles have the same area? What patterns can you find?

Length (cm)					
Width (cm)					
Perimeter (cm)					
Area (cm²)					

9.3 Perimeters of rectangles and squares (2)

Learning objective

Calculate the perimeter of rectangles and squares

Basic questions

1 Find the perimeters of the following figures.

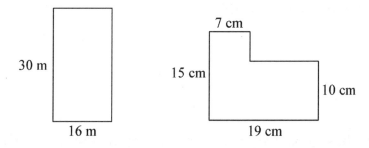

2 (a) Write the missing items of the rectangles in the table.

Length	Width	Perimeter	Area
	90 cm	480 cm	
19 cm			437 cm²
16 m	900 cm		

(b) Write the side length, perimeter and areas of the squares in the table.

Side length	Perimeter	Area
24 cm		
	1 m	

3 Tom put together five identical squares with side length of 8 cm to form a rectangle. Find the perimeter and the area of the rectangle. (Hint: first draw a diagram to help.)

4 A rectangular field is to be expanded. If the length is increased by 8 m, the area is increased by 160 m². If only the width is increased by 5 m, the area is increased by 175 m². Find the perimeter of the original rectangular field.

5 Mohan has a string that can form a square with sides exactly 18 cm long. If he wants to use the string to form a rectangle with length of 19 cm, how long will the width be?

Challenge and extension questions

6 Eight identical squares with side length of 6 cm are put together to form a rectangle.

(a) How many different rectangles can be formed?

(b) Find the perimeter of each possible rectangle.

7 The figure shows a rectangular piece of paper. If a square with maximum area is first cut from the paper, and then another square with maximum area is cut from the remaining rectangular piece, what are the area and perimeter of each square obtained? What are the area and perimeter of the remaining piece of paper? (unit: cm; drawing not to scale.)

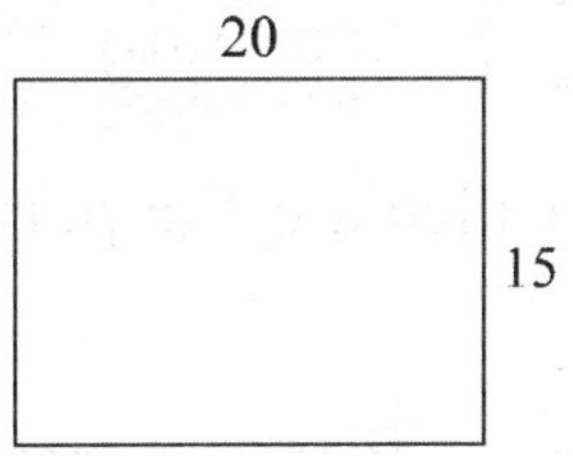

20

15

9.4 Perimeters and areas of rectilinear shapes

 Learning objective

Calculate the perimeters and areas of rectilinear shapes

 Basic questions

1. Calculate the perimeters and areas of the following figures. (The side length of each small square is 2 cm.)

(a)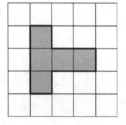

The perimeter＝(   )

The area＝(   )

(b)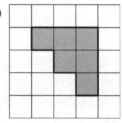

The perimeter＝(   )

The area＝(   )

(c)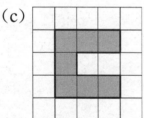

The perimeter＝(   )

The area＝(   )

(d)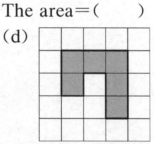

The perimeter＝(   )

The area＝(   )

2. Calculate the areas and the perimeters of the following figures. (unit: cm)

(a)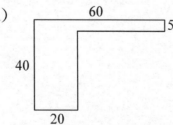

(b)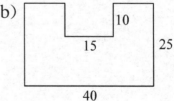

188

3 The figure below shows a rectangle. Given that the perimeter of the rectangle is 66 cm, find its area.

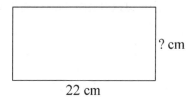

? cm

22 cm

4 The figure shows a square. Its perimeter is 108 m. What is its area?

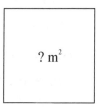

? m²

5 Jeremy and Michael each have a wire of the same length. Jeremy has bent his wire into a rectangle of length 9 cm and width 3 cm. Michael wants to bend his wire to form a square. What will be the area of the square Michael gets?

 Challenge and extension questions

6 The shaded part in the figure below is the overlap of two identical rectangles. (unit: cm)

(a) Find the area of the unshaded part in the figure.

(b) Find the perimeter of the whole figure.

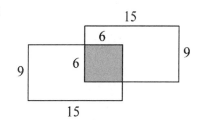

15

6

9

6

9

6

15

7 The perimeter of a rectangle is 240 cm. If both the length and the width are increased by 50 cm, by how many square centimetres is the area increased? (Hint: first draw a diagram to help.)

8 The figure shows a rectangle which is inside a square. The side length of the square is 18 cm. The four vertices of the rectangle divide each side of the square into two parts. The longer part is twice the length of the shorter part. How many square centimetres is the area of this rectangle?

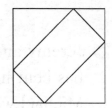

9.5 Describing positions on a 2-D grid

 Learning objective

Describe positions and movements on a 2-D grid

 Basic questions

1. The diagram below shows the arrangement of seating positions in a cinema. Please help the children find their seats. (Draw a line to match.)

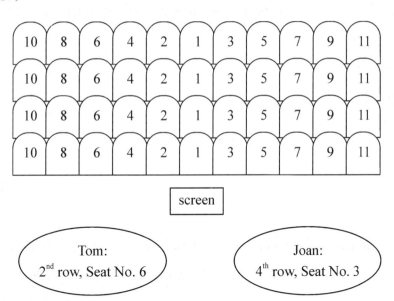

10	8	6	4	2	1	3	5	7	9	11
10	8	6	4	2	1	3	5	7	9	11
10	8	6	4	2	1	3	5	7	9	11
10	8	6	4	2	1	3	5	7	9	11

screen

Tom:
2nd row, Seat No. 6

Joan:
4th row, Seat No. 3

2. Think carefully and fill in the blanks. (Hint: choose 'horizontally' or 'vertically'.)

When looking for the position on a location map, we first locate it _____ , and then locate it _____ .

3. Fill in the brackets to indicate the position of each animal on the grid. The first one has been done for you.

5	Cow							Monkey		
4				Rabbit						
3			Tiger			Sheep				
2				Horse						Dog
1									Cat	
	1	2	3	4	5	6	7	8	9	10

Cow (_1_ , _5_)   Tiger (___ , ___)   Rabbit (___ , ___)
Horse (___ , ___)   Sheep (___ , ___)   Monkey (___ , ___)
Cat (___ , ___)   Dog (___ , ___)

4 Mark the place where each flower belongs on the grid below.

Lily (2, 1)

Iris (6, 3)

Tulip (3, 7)

Rose (5, 4)

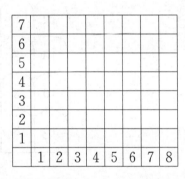

5 A snail is at (2, 9) on the grid below. It moves first 6 squares right,
then 7 squares down, then 4 squares left, and finally 3 squares up.

(a) What position does the snail finally reach?

(b) Are there other routes for the snail to move to the same final position? If so, please describe two such routes.

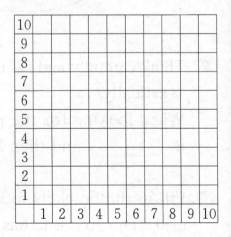

Challenge and extension question

6 The diagram below shows a street map on a grid.

(a) If the position of the post office is described as (1, 5), then the position of the supermarket is (____ , ____).

(b) There are _____ shortest routes from the post office to the supermarket.

Post office

Supermarket

9.6 Solving problems involving time and money (1)

📖 **Learning objective**

Solve problems involving time

✏️ **Basic questions**

① Fill in the brackets.
   (a) There are (   ) months in a year.
   (b) There are (   ) days in a common year and (   ) days in a leap year.
   (c) There are (   ) days in February in a common year and (   ) days in a leap year.
   (d) There are (   ) days in the first three months of this year.

② Write a suitable number in the brackets.
   (a) 1 hour＝(   ) minutes＝(   ) seconds
   (b) 1.5 hours＝(   ) minutes
   (c) $\frac{3}{4}$ hour＝(   ) minutes＝(   ) seconds
   (d) 45 minutes＝ (   ) hours
   (e) 190 minutes＝(   ) hours and (   ) minutes
   (f) 2.5 days ＝(   ) hours
   (g) 3 weeks＝(   ) days＝(   ) hours
   (h) $\frac{1}{2}$ year＝(   ) months

③ Look at each clock face below. What time does it represent? Write your answer to the nearest minute and in both 12-hour and 24-hour formats.

Analogue 12-hour clock

In 12-hour format: _____

In 24-hour format: _____

Digital 24-hour clock

In 12-hour format: _____

In 24-hour format: _____

Analogue 12-hour clock

In 12-hour format: _____

In 24-hour format: _____

Digital 24-hour clock

In 12-hour format: _____

In 24-hour format: _____

4 A football game started at 18:30. It lasted 135 minutes. When did the game end?

5 A bicycle shop sold 1365 bikes in 15 weeks.

(a) How many bikes did the shop sell on average each day and each week?

(b) If each bike is sold at £95 on average, what is the total amount of money that the shop received from selling all the bikes each day and each week?

(c) If the shop makes a profit of £28 by selling one bicycle on average, how much profit did it make each day and each week?

 Challenge and extension questions

6 In 24 hours, how many full rotations does the hour hand move on the clock face? How many full rotations does the minute hand move on the clock face?

7 Julia's family used 15 kilowatt-hours (kWh) of electricity per day in the last year.

(a) How many kilowatt-hours did her family use in the first 6 months of that year?

(b) If it costs 12 pence per kWh, how much does the family need to pay per day? How much did the family need to pay for the first 6 month in the last year? Express your answers in whole pounds and pence.

9.7 Solving problems involving time and money (2)

 Learning objective

Solve problems involving money and time

 Basic questions

1. Fill in the brackets with a suitable number. (Hint: use a whole number, fraction or decimal.)

   (a) £1＝(   ) pence

   (b) £$\frac{1}{10}$＝(   ) pence

   (c) 60p＝(   ) pounds

   (d) £$\frac{3}{4}$＝(   ) pence

   (e) 890p＝(   ) pounds and (   ) pence

   (f) 1p＝(   ) pound

   (g) £80.50＝(   ) pence

   (h) £2.38＝(   ) pence

2. Fill in the blanks.
   (a) A school bought 600 ropes. This cost £3600. Each rope cost (   ) pounds.
   (b) Each volleyball costs £50. Mr Lee can only buy (   ) volleyballs with £150.
   (c) Each ball costs £9. Mr Lee bought 72 balls. He paid (   ) pounds.

3. A gardening shop sold 12 bags of garden gravel and 4 bags of bark chippings in a day. Each bag of gravel was priced at £4 and each bag of bark chippings was priced at £75. What was the total amount of money received from the sales?

4 Emily has graduated from university and her monthly salary is £2512. Her younger brother, Martin, works part-time during school terms and earns an hourly wage of £9.50.

(a) What is Emily's annual salary?

(b) In the August school holidays, Martin works full time for 8 hours per day, 5 days per week. Given the hourly wage is the same, can you estimate and then calculate how much he earns in a week? What is the difference between your estimate and the actual amount he earns?

(c) Are Martin's earnings in four weeks when woorking full time more or less than half of Emily's monthly salary?

5 Anna and her family went on holiday for three weeks. They spent £5418 in total.

(a) How much on average did they spend per day and per week, respectively?

(b) If the family cut down their holiday to two weeks and keep the daily cost the same, how much money could they save?

Challenge and extension questions

6 A pancake vendor sold 6 pancakes per minute in an evening. The pancakes were 99 pence each. If the vendor started working from 17:45 and ended at 19:05, how many pounds did he get from pancake sales that evening?

7 A new school plans to buy desks and chairs for 14 classes. A desk and chair set costs £15. Each class needs 30 sets of desks and chairs. If the school has a budget of £6500 for these two items, is it enough to make the purchase? By how much is the budget more or less than the total purchase price?

Unit test 9

1 Fill in the brackets.

(a) 90 000 m = (   ) km

(b) 3.5 km = (   ) km and (   ) m

(c) One lap around a running track is 200 m. Eight laps are (   ) km.

(d) The distance between London and Glasgow is about 556 (   ). (Choose: km, m or cm.)

(e) The perimeter of a square is 4 times (   ).

(f) The perimeter of a rectangle is twice the sum of (   ) and (   ).

(g) $\frac{1}{2}$ day = (   ) hours = (   ) minutes.

(h) 250p = (   ) pounds = (   ) pounds and (   ) pence.

2 Calculate and then fill in the brackets.

(a) A rectangle has a length of 1 metre and width of 80 cm. Its perimeter is (   ) m or (   ) cm.

(b) If three identical squares with a side length of 40 cm are put together to form a rectangle, the perimeter of this rectangle is (   ).

(c) If the side length of each small square is 1 m, the perimeter of the shaded part is (   ) and its area is (   ). (drawing not to scale.)

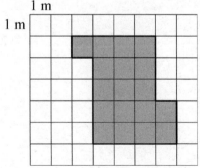

1 m

1 m

❸ Complete the tables.

(a)

Rectangle	Length	Width	Perimeter
	7 m	9 m	
	90 cm		280 cm
		8 cm	40 cm

(b)

Square	Side length	Perimeter
	24 m	
		24 m
	90 cm	

4 True or false.

(a) There are 365 days in each year. ( )

(b) 705p is equal to £7.5. ( )

(c) If the perimeters of two rectangles are equal, then their areas must be equal too. ( )

(d) If the side length of a square is increased by 4 times, its area is increased by 16 times. ( )

❺ Find the perimeter and the area of the figure below. (unit: cm; drawing not to scale.)

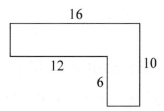

6 Craig was standing at $(7, 2)$ on the grid below. He then walked 3 squares left and 5 squares up. Then he walked another 4 squares right, and 2 squares down. At what position did he end up?

7									
6									
5									
4									
3									
2									
1									
	1	2	3	4	5	6	7	8	9

7 Application problems.

(a) A rectangular sports field has a width of 400 m, which is 250 m shorter than its length. Daniel walked three complete laps of the field. What is the total distance he walked? Express your answer first in metres and then in kilometres.

(b) The perimeter of a square piece of iron sheet is 100 cm. Find its area.

(c) If the width of a rectangular field is reduced by 5 m while the length is unchanged, its area is reduced by 100 m^2. If the length is increased by 6 m while the width is unchanged, its area is increased by 90 m^2. What is the area of this rectangular field? (Hint: first draw a diagram to help.)

(d) A rectangular piece of green land has a length of 80 m and a width of 60 m. A 3-metre-wide path is built outwards around the edge of the green land. What is the area of the path?

(e) The side length of Square A is 8 cm longer than that of Square B. The area of Square B is 384 cm^2 less than that of Square A. What are the areas of Square A and Square B?

(f) Mary saved £828 in the last year.
  (i) How much did she save in each month on average?

  (ii) If Mary saved £118 in the first two months, how much did she save monthly on average in the rest of the year?

(g) A toy shop sold seven toy cars per day on average in August and September.
  (i) How many toy cars did it sell from 30 August to 10 September?

  (ii) If each toy car is sold for £25, how much money did the shop receive each day on average from selling the toy cars? How much money did it receive in the above period?

(h) A printer prints 15 pages per minute.

(i) If it started printing from 12:45 and ended at 1:13 pm on a day, how many pages did the printer print?

(ii) If the printing cost is 12p per page, how much did printing all the pages cost? (Express your answer first in pence and then in pounds.)

Chapter 10 Four operations of whole numbers

10.1 Calculating work efficiency (1)

Learning objective

Use multiplication and division to solve rate problems

Basic questions

1 The table below shows the numbers of toys that three workers, Mr. Lee, Mr. Wood and Mr. Edge made in different numbers of days.

	Mr. Lee	Mr. Wood	Mr. Edge
Number of toys	252	215	360
Number of days	6	5	8

Please read the table carefully. From the table, do you know who was the fastest in making toys? The numbers of toys and time are all different. How can we compare them?

2 In the question above, the number of toys that Mr. Lee, Mr. Wood and Mr. Edge made per day can be termed **work efficiency**. In general, **work efficiency** is the amount of work completed divided by the time taken. Fill in the ○ with '×' or '÷'.

(a) work efficiency＝amount of work ○ time taken

(b) amount of work＝ work efficiency ○ ☐

(c) time taken＝ amount of work ○ ☐

3 Write the number sentences and then calculate.

(a) Lily has read 132 pages of a book in four days. How many pages did she read per day?

(b) Tom can do 32 mental sums per minute. With the same efficiency, how many mental sums can he do in 5 minutes?

(c) Camilla can assemble 30 pieces of parts per hour. With the same efficiency, how many hours does it take her to assemble 480 pieces of parts?

(d) Adam and Tony took part in voluntary work in school for stuffing envelopes. Adam stuffed 270 envelopes in three hours. Tony stuffed 400 envelopes in five hours. Who has higher work efficiency?

Challenge and extension questions

4 Joan did 216 skips in 3 minutes. With the same rate, how many minutes would it take her to do 144 more skips?

5 A 1200-metre-long road needs to be repaired. Company A can finish the job in 40 days. Company B can finish it in 30 days. How many more metres can Company B repair than Company B per day?

10.2 Calculating work efficiency (2)

Learning objective

Use multiplication and division to solve rate problems

Basic questions

1 Draw a tree diagram according to the question. Then write the number sentences and calculate. The first one has been done for you.

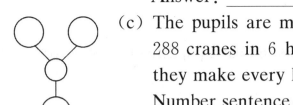

(a) The pupils are making paper cranes. They can make 50 cranes per hour. How many paper cranes can they make in 3 hours?

Number sentence: $50 \times 3 = 150$

Answer: They can make 150 paper cranes in 3 hours.

(b) The pupils are making paper cranes. They can make 50 cranes per hour. How many hours do they need to make 1000 paper cranes?

Number sentence: _____

Answer: _____

(c) The pupils are making paper cranes. If they made 288 cranes in 6 hours, how many paper cranes did they make every hour on average?

Number sentence: _____

Answer: _____

2 Application problems.

(a) A community school planned to save 18 kilowatts of electricity every day. Now they have saved 4 more kilowatts of electricity every day than they planned. At this rate, how many kilowatts can they save in total for a month? (Note: take a month as 22 days.)

(b) Jane, Cathy and Emmy worked in a bag factory. Jane made 18 bags in 3 hours. Cathy made 14 bags in 2 hours. Emmy made 20 bags in 4 hours. Who made the most bags per hour?

(c) A factory received an order to process a batch of parts. They had processed 6480 pieces of parts, which was 8 times as many as the unprocessed parts. How many pieces of parts were there in the batch?

Challenge and extension question

3 There are 4 classes in Year 4. Each class has 30 pupils. In 20 days, the pupils have read 9600 co-curricular books altogether.
(a) How many co-curricular books did each class read on average?

(b) How many co-curricular books did each pupil read on average?

(c) How many co-curricular books did the pupils read altogether every day on average?

(d) How many co-curricular books did each pupil read every day on average?

10.3 Solving calculation questions in 3 steps (1)

Learning objective

Calculate using mixed operations and brackets

Basic questions

1. Fill in the blanks.
   (a) When you work on a number sentence with brackets, perform calculations inside the brackets first.
   For example, $(2+3) \times (6-2) = \underline{\qquad}$.
   (b) When you work on a number sentence involving four operations, perform all the multiplication and division first and then perform the addition and subtraction.
   For example, $18 \div 2 + 3 \times 5 = \underline{\qquad}$.
   (c) When you work on a number sentence only with multiplication and division, work from left to right.
   For example, $20 \div 5 \times 4 = \underline{\qquad}$.
   (d) When you work on a number sentence only with addition and subtraction, work from left to right.
   For example, $18 - 2 + 11 = \underline{\qquad}$.

2. Work them out mentally. Write the answers.
   (a) $4 \times 5 + 4 =$
   (b) $6 \div 3 + 12 =$
   (c) $12 + 12 \div 4 =$
   (d) $10 \times 2 - 7 =$
   (e) $13 - 5 \times 2 =$
   (f) $(7-3) \times 6 =$
   (g) $9 \div 9 + 12 =$
   (h) $9 + 8 + 7 =$
   (i) $10 \div (5+5) =$

3. Have you ever played a poker game called '24 points'? It is a number game; you are shown a set of four cards with numbers and required to use addition, subtraction, multiplication and division

(including brackets) to get 24 points. (Cards A, J, Q and K represent 1, 11, 12 and 13 respectively.)

Let's play the game. One method has been done for you.

(a)

Calculation method 1: $(5×6)-8+2=24$

Calculation method 2: _____

(b)

Calculation method 1: _____

Calculation method 2: _____

4 Insert $+$, $-$, $×$, $÷$ and ( ) in each set of numbers below so the result is 24.

(a) 4   2   6   3=

(b) 3   6   4   2=

(c) 3   6   2   4=

(d) 2   6   3   4=

5 In each set of four numbers, insert $+$, $-$, $×$, $÷$ and ( ) in the numbers so that the result is 24. (Each number can be used only once.)

(a) 7, 7, 1, 2

(b) 6, 2, 7, 4

(c) 12, 8, 6, 4

(d) 1, 12, 10, 13

Challenge and extension questions

6 Can the four numbers in each set below make 24 using four operations and brackets?

(a) 4, 4, 4, 4 ·· ( )

(b) 5, 5, 5, 5 ··· ( )

(c) 8, 8, 8, 8 ··· ( )

(d) 9, 9, 9, 9 ··· ( )

(e) 12, 12, 12, 12 ··· ( )

7 Fill in the nine boxes with the numbers $1-9$ to make the equations true. Each number can be used only once.

(a) $6 \times (\boxed{} - 8) = 6$

(b) $(\boxed{} + 6) \div 2 = 5$

(c) $\boxed{} \div 3 + 1 = 3$

(d) $3 \times \boxed{} + \boxed{} = 16$

(e) $\boxed{} \times \boxed{} - 15 = 9$

(f) $2 \times (\boxed{} - \boxed{}) = 10$

10.4　Solving calculation questions in 3 steps (2)

 Learning objective

Calculate using mixed operations and brackets

 Basic questions

1 Write the number sentences with mixed operations according to the tree diagrams. The first one has been done for you.

(a)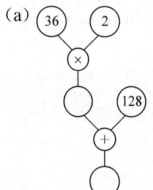

Number sentence:
$(36 \times 2) + 128 = 200$

(b)

Number sentence:

_____

(c)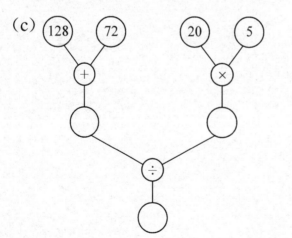

Number sentence: _____

2 Multiple choice questions.

(a) The correct order of operations to calculate $600+600\div 25\times 4$ is (   ).

A. Addition→division→multiplication

B. Division→addition→multiplication

C. Multiplication→addition→division

D. Division→multiplication→addition

(b) The result of $492-66\div 3\times 22$ is (   ).

A. 451   B. 8   C. 157   D. 2904

3 In each question below, put the calculations in three steps into one number sentence with mixed operations and then calculate.

(a) $650\div 50=13$
$13+45=58$
$58+60=118$

(b) $35\times 6=210$
$121\div 11=11$
$210-11=199$

Number sentence: _____   Number sentence: _____

4 Give the order of operations first and then work it out step by step.

(a) $462\div 3+66\div 22$ (b) $66-480\div 20\div 3$

(c) $947+150\times 24\div 30$ (d) $993-2600\div 8+549$

Challenge and extension questions

5 Put the calculations in four steps into one number sentence with mixed operations and then calculate.

$7\times 9=63$ $142\div 2=71$ $71-63=8$ $8+2=10$

Number sentence: _____

6 A vertical bamboo pole is used to measure the depth of the water. The part above the water is 120 cm long, which is 20 cm less than twice the part in the water. How deep is the water?

10.5 Solving calculation questions in 3 steps (3)

 Learning objective

Calculate using mixed operations and brackets

 Basic questions

1 Put the calculations in three steps into one number sentence with mixed operations and then calculate.

(a) $650 \div 50 = 13$
$45 - 20 = 25$
$25 + 13 = 38$

Number sentence: _____

(b) $35 - 23 = 12$
$121 + 11 = 132$
$132 \div 12 = 11$

Number sentence: _____

2 Give the order of operations first and then work it out step by step.

(a) $24 - 0 \div 24 + 24$

(b) $240 + 240 \div (240 - 200)$

(c) $160 \div (39 + 36 \div 36)$

(d) $(450 - 133 + 23) \times 18$

(e) $44 \times 60 \div (8 \times 5)$

(f) $205 - 330 \div (307 - 277)$

3 Fill in the blanks.

(a) If a number sentence contains multiplication and division, as well as addition and subtraction but without brackets, then we first do _____ and then do _____.

(b) If a number sentence contains brackets, then we first do _____.

(c) For $(6400-800 \times 20) \div 4$, the correct order of operations is to do _____ first, then _____ and finally _____.

4 Application problems.

(a) A school is organising a field trip for 42 teachers and 567 pupils. Each coach can seat 40 people. Everyone must be seated. How many coaches are needed for the trip?

(b) In a supermarket, 22 boxes of apples were sold in the morning and 34 boxes in the afternoon. The weight of the apples that were sold in the afternoon was 360 kilograms more than that of the apples sold in the morning.

(i) How many kilograms does each box of apples weigh?

(ii) How many kilograms of apples have been sold in total?

(iii) If the price for each box of apples is £80, how much did the supermarket receive on that day from selling these boxes of apples?

Challenge and extension questions

5 Put brackets in each of the following number sentences to make the equation true.

$480 - 360 \div 12 + 8 = 6$ $480 - 360 \div 12 + 8 = 462$

6 There were 724 books in a school library. Year 1 pupils borrowed 88 books. Year 2 pupils borrowed half of the remaining books. The other half of the remaining books were shared equally by Year 3, Year 4 and Year 5. How many books did Year 4 pupils receive?

10.6　Solving calculation questions in 3 steps (4)

 Learning objective

Calculate using mixed operations and brackets

 Basic questions

1　Write the number sentences with mixed operations according to the tree diagrams.

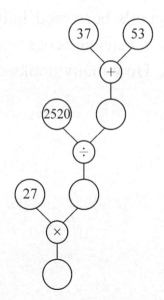

Number sentence: _____

2　Put the calculations in three steps into one number sentence with mixed operations and then calculate.

(a) $247 - 82 = 165$
$\quad 165 \times 2 = 330$
$\quad 660 \div 330 = 2$
Number sentence: _____

(b) $70 + 20 = 90$
$\quad 1000 - 90 = 910$
$\quad 910 \times 2 = 1820$
Number sentence: _____

3 Fill in the brackets.

(a) If a number sentence has round brackets inside square brackets, then you perform the calculation first within (　　　) and then (　　　). For example, $10+[5\times(6\div3)]=($ 　 $)$.

(b) In $29\times[1440\div(328-280)]$, the correct order of calculations is to do the subtraction first, then (　　　) and finally (　　　).

(c) In $[(1400\div2)-(328+280)]\times2$, the correct order of calculations is to do (　　　) first or (　　　), then (　　　) and finally (　　　).

(d) In a subtraction sentence, if the minuend is 25 greater than the subtrahend and 52 greater than the difference, then the minuend is (　　).

(e) 2000 kg 550 g$-$1100 g$=($ 　 $)$ kg.

4 Give the order of operations first and then work it out step by step.

(a) $155-(4160\div20-86)$　　(b) $[846+(56-32)\times16]\div30$

(c) $8000\div[800-(560+40)]$　(d) $3205-4020\div(301-281)$

(e) $[3180-(79+101)]\div40$　(f) $2430\div[(2200-1480)\div8]$

Challenge and extension question

5 A barrel of oil weighs 21 kilograms, including the weight of the barrel. After using $\frac{1}{3}$ of the oil, it weighs 15 kilograms including the barrel. What is the weight of the barrel?

10.7 Working forward

Learning objective

Calculate using mixed operations

Basic questions

1 Complete the tree diagram based on the diagram on the left. Write the number sentence and then calculate.

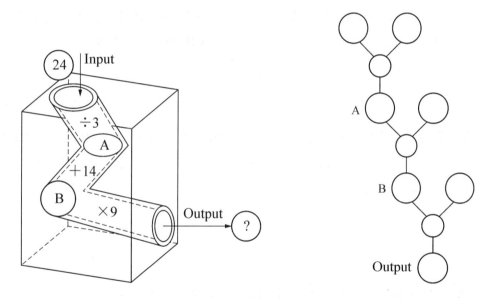

Number sentence: _____

2 Fill in the brackets. Then write the number sentence with mixed operations and calculate.

(a) $1000 \xrightarrow{\div 5} (\quad) \xrightarrow{-118} (\quad) \xrightarrow{\times 2} (\quad)$

Number sentence: _____

(b) $1285 \xrightarrow{-892} (\quad) \xrightarrow{-369} (\quad) \xrightarrow{\div 8} (\quad)$

Number sentence: _____

3 Write the number sentence and then calculate.

(a) First add 2 to 17, then multiply it by 2, and finally subtract 2. What is the result?

(b) 71 is subtracted by 2 times 15, and then multiplied by 24. What is the result?

4 Application problems.

(a) There were 12 passengers on a bus when it departed. 2 passengers got off and 6 passengers got on the bus at the first stop. At the second stop, 3 passengers got off and 4 passengers got on. How many passengers were then on the bus?

(b) A farm has 360 geese. The number of chicken is 32 more than 3 times the number of geese. How many chickens does the farm have?

Challenge and extension questions

5 Grandpa is 68 years old. Half of Grandpa's age plus 8 is 3 times Mary's age. How old is Mary?

6 Start with zero, followed by operations of first adding 6 and then subtracting 2. Repeat this process. After how many operations will the result be 26? (Adding 6 and subtracting 2 are considered two operations.)

10.8 Working backward

Learning objective

Calculate using mixed operations

Basic questions

1 Complete the tree diagram based on the diagram on the left. Write the number sentence and then calculate.

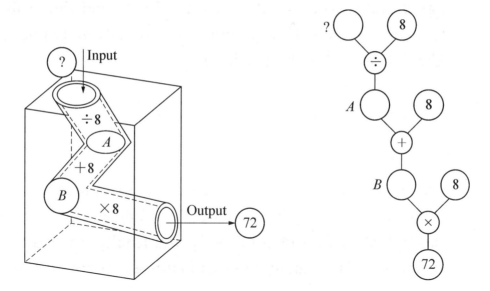

Number sentence: _____

2 Fill in the brackets. Then write the number sentence with mixed operations and calculate.

(a) (?) $\xrightarrow{+34}$ ( ) $\xrightarrow{\times 3}$ ( ) $\xrightarrow{-190}$ 149

Number sentence: _____

(b) (?) $\xrightarrow{\div 23}$ ( ) $\xrightarrow{-76}$ ( ) $\xrightarrow{\times 50}$ 750

Number sentence: _____

3 Write the number sentence and then calculate.

(a) After a number is added by 8 and then multiplied by 8, it is 160. What is the number?

(b) Five times a number is equal to 20 less than 8 times 45. What is the number?

4 Application problems.

(a) In a maths activity, the teacher said to the pupils: 'After my age is added to by 4, then divided by 3, and then subtracted from by 14, and finally multiplied by 20, it happens to be 100.' How old is the teacher?

(b) There are many pomegranates on a pomegranate tree. If the number of the pomegranates is subtracted from by 7, multiplied by 7, added to by 7, and finally divided by 7, the result is 7. How many pomegranates are there on the tree?

Challenge and extension questions

5 In $\boxed{} \times 8 \div 5 - 24 = 48$, what number should be in the $\boxed{}$?

6 John was reading a storybook. On the first say, he read 6 pages more than half of the book. On the second day, he read 5 pages more than half of the remaining part of the book. There were 13 pages left. How many pages were there in the book?

10.9 Word calculation problems (1)

 Learning objective

Solve word problems involving mixed operations

Basic questions

1 Think carefully. Fill in the brackets, write the number sentences and calculate.

(a) The quotient of 150 divided by 6 is multiplied by 12. What is the product?

The equation for the quantitative relationship is:

Product=(   )×(   ).

Number sentences: _____

(b) The sum of 288 and 42 is divided by 30. What is the quotient?

The equation for the quantitative relationship is:

Quotient=(   )÷(   ).

Number sentences: _____

2 Multiple choice question. Read each question carefully. Fill in each bracket with the letter of the correct number sentence on the next page.

(a) What is the sum of 108 and the product of 32 and 23?

Answer: (   )

(b) What is the product of the sum of 108 and 32 multiplied by 23?

Answer: (   )

(c) What is the product of 108 multiplied by the sum of 32 and 23?

Answer: (   )

(d) What is the quotient of 108 divided by the difference of 32 and 23?   Answer: (　　)

    A. $108 \times (32 + 23)$ B. $(108 + 32) \times 23$

    C. $108 + 32 \times 23$ D. $108 \div (32 - 23)$

3 Write the number sentences and then calculate.

(a) What is the sum of the quotient of 600 divided by 20 and 187?

(b) What is the quotient of the product of 500 and 32 divided by 100?

(c) What is the difference between the product of 470 and 15 and the product of 17 and 104?

(d) The dividend is 244. The divisor is 118 less than half of the dividend. What is the quotient?

(e) What is the difference between 1098 and half of 756?

Challenge and extension questions

4 There are three numbers 0, 2 and 8. They form a greatest 3-digit number and a least 3-digit number. What is their product?

5 Tom is 9 years old. His father is 37 years old. How old will Tom be when his father's age is 3 times his age?

10.10 Word calculation problems (2)

Learning objective

Solve word problems involving mixed operations

Basic questions

1 Think carefully. Fill in the brackets, write the number sentences and calculate.

(a) The quotient of 210 divided by 7 is multiplied by the difference between 120 and 80. What is the product?

The equation for the quantitative relationship is:

Product=(   )×(   ).

Number sentence: _____

(b) What is the sum of the product of 34 and 12 and the quotient of 48 divided by 12?

The equation for the quantitative relationship is:

Sum=(   )+(   ).

Number sentences: _____

2 Write the number sentences and then calculate.

(a) The sum of 66 twenty-fives is divided by the sum of 6 fives. What is the quotient?

(b) Number B is 2940, which is 20 times Number A. How much more is Number B than Number A?

228

(c) A number is divided by 50. The quotient is 128 and the remainder is 36. Find the number.

(d) How much less is the quotient of 6300 divided by 60 than two times 72?

3 Multiple choice questions. Read each question carefully. Fill in the brackets with the letter of the correct number sentence.

(a) What is the difference between the product of 6 and 78 and the quotient of 20 divided by 2? (   )

(b) The difference between 78 and half of 20 is multiplied by 6. What is the result? (   )

(c) The difference of the product of 6 and 78 subtracted by 20 is divided by 2. What is the quotient? (   )

(d) The product of 6 and the difference between 78 and 20 is divided by 2. What is the result? (   )

      A. $(78-20 \div 2) \times 6$ B. $6 \times (78-20) \div 2$

      C. $6 \times 78 - 20 \div 2$ D. $(6 \times 78 - 20) \div 2$

Challenge and extension questions

4 Express the following number sentences in words and then calculate.

(a) $403 \times (213-90) - 13$ (b) $864 \div [(2193-1473) \div 90]$

5 The sum of 4 times a number and 456 is 1000. What is the number?

10.11　Laws of operations (1)

Learning objective

Use the commutative and associative laws to calculate efficiently

Basic questions

1　Fill in the brackets.

(a) When adding two numbers, we can swap the (　　) of the two addends and their sum remains (　　　　). This is known as the **commutative law of addition**. Using letters a and b to represent the two addends, it is: $a + b = ($　　$) + ($　　$)$.

(b) When multiplying two numbers, we can swap the (　　) of the two factors and their product remains (　　). This is known as the **commutative law of multiplication**. Using letters a and b to represent the two factors, it is: $a \times b = ($　　$) \times ($　　$)$.

(c) When adding three numbers, we can add the first two numbers first and then add the third number or add the last two numbers first and then add the first number. The sum remains (　　). This is known as the **associative law of addition**. Using letters a, b and c to represent the three numbers, it is: $(a + b) + c = a + ($　　$)$.

(d) When multiplying three numbers, we can multiply the first two numbers first and then multiply the third number or multiply the last two numbers first and then multiply the first number. The product remains (　　). This is known as the **associative law of multiplication**. Using letters a, b and c to represent the three numbers, it is: $(a \times b) \times c = a \times ($　　$)$.

2　Fill in the blanks using the laws of operations.

(a) $732 + 488 = 488 + $_____

230

(b) $379 + 248 + 621 = 379 + \underline{\hspace{2cm}} + \underline{\hspace{2cm}}$

(c) $26 \times 14 = \underline{\hspace{2cm}} \times 26$

(d) $250 \times 27 \times 4 = 27 \times (\underline{\hspace{2cm}} \times \underline{\hspace{2cm}})$

(e) $\triangle + \star = \underline{\hspace{2cm}} + \underline{\hspace{2cm}}$

(f) $\circledcirc \times \diamondsuit = \underline{\hspace{2cm}} \times \underline{\hspace{2cm}}$

(g) $x + y + z = x + (\underline{\hspace{2cm}} + \underline{\hspace{2cm}})$

(h) $j \times k \times l = j \times (\underline{\hspace{2cm}} \times \underline{\hspace{2cm}})$

3 Use the column method to calculate the following. Check your answers by using the commutative law of addition and that of multiplication.

(a) $1736 + 839$ (b) $675 + 868$

(c) 57×143 (d) 507×69

4 Simplify and then calculate.

(a) $169 + 226 + 274$ (b) $(923 + 174) + 26$

(c) $(75 \times 25) \times 4$ (d) $2 \times 34 \times 50$

(e) $357 + 432 + 368 + 153$ (f) $13 \times 125 \times 7 \times 8$

Challenge and extension question

5 Simplify each of the following calculations and then find the answer.

(a) $385 - 173 + 615 - 227$ (b) $16 \times (125 \times 6)$

(c) $9 + 98 + 997 + 9996 + 99\,995 + 999\,994 + 21$

10.12 Laws of operations (2)

 Learning objective

Use the commutative and associative laws to calculate efficiently

 Basic questions

1 Fill in the brackets using the laws of operations.

(a) (   ) $+ 270 = 270 + 80$

(b) $25 \times 976 = 976 \times ($)

(c) (   ) $+ 56 = ($) $+ 44$

(d) $a + ($) $= b + ($)

(e) $(a + \underline{\quad\quad}) + c = a + (b + \underline{\quad\quad})$

(f) $(a \times \underline{\quad\quad}) \times c = a \times (b \times \underline{\quad\quad})$

(g) $(33 + 16) + 84 = ($) $+ (16 + \underline{\quad\quad})$

(h) (   ) $\times \blacktriangle = ($) $\times \blacksquare$

(i) $75 \times 8 \times 2 \times 125 = (\underline{\quad} \times \underline{\quad}) \times (\underline{\quad} \times \underline{\quad})$

2 Simplify and then calculate.

(a) $37 + 128 + 53 + 72 + 10$ (b) $25 \times 8 \times 125 \times 4$

(c) 25×64 (d) $(125 \times 6) \times 72$

(e) 125×88 (f) $7 \times 125 \times 25 \times 32$

3 Application problems.

(a) Each piece of cake costs £6. Each box has 4 pieces of cake. How much do 25 boxes of cake cost? (Use two methods to calculate.)

(b) Five boxes of erasers cost £40. Each box has 4 erasers. How much does each eraser cost? (Use two methods to calculate.)

(c) A big event's flower team wanted to organise a rectangular parade. The parade consists of 25 rows, with 8 people in each row. Each person holds two flowers. How many flowers are needed for the flower team?

Challenge and extension question

4 Calculate smartly.

(a) $625 \times 8 \times 8 \times 2 \times 2 \times 2$

(b) There are ( ) zeros at the end of the product $1 \times 2 \times 3 \times 4 \times 5 \times \cdots \times 28 \times 29 \times 30$.

10.13 Laws of operations (3)

 Learning objective

Use the distributive law to calculate efficiently

Basic questions

1 Calculate and then draw a line to match each pair.

(a) $10 \times 3 + 10 \times 9$ A. $23 \times (7 + 8 + 5)$

(b) $42 \times 8 - 4 \times 42$ B. $(8 - 4) \times 42$

(c) $23 \times 7 + 23 \times 8 + 23 \times 5$ C. $10 \times (3 + 9)$

(d) Please write two more pairs of number sentences like these.

_____

_____

(e) Please use letters to express the **distributive law of multiplication over addition** and the **distributive law of multiplication over subtraction.**

_____

2 Fill in each blank with a suitable number and each $\bigcirc$ with an operation sign.

(a) $49 + 36 + $ _____ $= $ _____ $+ (36 \bigcirc 64)$

(b) $\stackrel{\wedge}{\sim} \times \triangle \times$ _____ $= \stackrel{\wedge}{\sim} \times (\triangle \bigcirc \square)$

(c) $(42 + 35) \times$ _____ $= $ _____ $\times 15 + $ _____ $\times 15$

(d) $a \times c \bigcirc$ _____ $\times$ _____ $= (c - d) \times a$

(e) $22 \times 55 - 11 \times 55 = $ _____ $\times ($ _____ $\bigcirc$ _____ $)$

(f) $43 \times 100 = 43 \times 27 \bigcirc 43 \times$ _____

3 True or false.

(a) $46 + 54 \times 77 = (46 + 54) \times 77$ (   )

(b) $25 \times 125 + 4 \times 8 = 25 \times 4 + 125 \times 8$ (   )

(c) $24 + 6 \times 36 = 6 \times (4 + 36)$ (   )

(d) $(125 + 71) \times 8 = (125 \times 8) + 71$ (   )

(e) $100 - 33 - 55 = 100 - (33 + 55)$ (   )

(f) $99 \times 99 + 99 = 99 \times 100$ (   )

4 Simplify each calculation below and then find the answer. Give the law of operations used.

(a) $78 \times 92 + 78 \times 8$ (b) $127 \times 24 - 24 \times 27$

(c) $(25 + 20) \times 4$ (d) $(125 - 30) \times 80$

(e) $39 \times 56 + 56 \times 13 + 5 \times 56$ (f) $24 \times 45 - 45 \times 9 + 85 \times 45$

(g) 43×99 (h) 207×101

Challenge and extension question

5 Someone made a careless mlstake in maths and calculated ($\boxed{} + 50) \times 4$ as $\boxed{} \times 4 + 50$. Do you know what the difference between the correct answer and the wrong answer is?

10.14   Laws of operations (4)

Learning objective

Use laws of operations to calculate efficiently

Basic questions

1 Fill in each bracket with the correct law of operations.

(a) In $315 + 438 + 185 + 562 = (315 + 185) + (438 + 562)$, (   ) are used.

(b) In $857 \times 25 \times 4 = 857 \times (25 \times 4)$, (   ) is used.

(c) In $8 \times 36 + 89 \times 8 = 8 \times (36 + 89)$, (   ) is used.

(d) In $(71 - 36) \times 20 = 71 \times 20 - 36 \times 20$, (   ) is used.

2 Use two different ways to simplify each of the following and then find the answer. Put a $\sqrt{}$ to indicate which method you prefer.

(a) 25×48 25×48

(b) 125×64 125×64

(c) 99×201 99×201

3 Simplify and then calculate.

(a) 101×59 (b) $35 + 35 \times 73 + 26 \times 35$

(c) $6 \times 127 + 71 \times 2 \times 3 + 12$ (d) $21 \times 96 + 84$

(e) $25 \times (8 + 4) \times 125$ (f) $25 \times (8 \times 4) \times 125$

4 Application problems.

(a) The passenger service information at a coach terminal is shown in the table below.

Type of coach	Number of trips per day	Average number of passengers on board
Regular coach	12	32
Mini coach	12	18

How many passengers were sent off from the terminal per day?

(b) There are 30 boxes of bananas and 4 boxes of apples in a fruit store. Each box weighs 25 kilograms. How many kilograms of fruit does the store have in total?

 Challenge and extension question

5 Calculate smartly.

(a) $280 \times 36 + 360 \times 72$ (b) $1999 + 999 \times 999$

10.15 Problem solving using four operations (1)

 Learning objective

Solve problems using four operations

 Basic questions

1 Think carefully, and fill in the brackets.

A company planned to build a 1200-metre auto-racing track in 40 days. It actually completed 10 more metres of the race track each day than planned.

(a) From the given condition 'to build 1200-metre auto-racing track in 40 days', we can find the planned work efficiency. The number sentence is (   ).

(b) From the given condition 'it actually completed 10 more metres of the race track each day than planned', we can find the actual work efficiency. The number sentence is (   ).

(c) Finally, from the given length of the auto-racing track and the actual work efficiency, we can find the actual amount of time taken to complete the work. The number sentence is (   ).

2 Application problems.

(a) A highway construction company planned to build a section of highway. According to the plan, it would build 91 metres of the highway per day, and complete the work in 10 days. It was actually completed in 7 days. How many metres of the highway were actually built each day? How many more metres were built each day than planned?

(b) A highway construction company planned to build a section of highway. According to the plan, it would build 81 metres per day and complete the work in 10 days. It actually built 9 metres more of the highway each day than it planned. How many days did the company actually take to complete the work? How many day(s) earlier did it complete the work than planned?

(c) A typist needs to type a 360-page manuscript. She planned to type 60 pages per day, but in fact she typed 90 pages per day. With the same efficiency, how many days earlier could she complete the task than planned?

(d) A typist needs to type a 360-page manuscript. She planned to finish the work in 6 days, but in fact she finished the work in 4 days. How many more pages did she type per day than planned?

(e) A school canteen has received 3000 kg of rice, which was planned to last for 20 days, but it actually lasted for 30 days. How many fewer kilograms of rice were consumed each day than originally expected?

(f) In 3 minutes, Mary can do 126 shuttlecock kicks and Cindy can do 135 shuttlecock kicks. How many more shuttlecock kicks can Cindy do than Mary per minute?

Challenge and extension questions

3 A factory needs to produce 3600 parts. If it is given to worker A, it will take 30 days. If it is given to worker B, it will take 20 days. If they work together to produce the parts, then in how many days can they finish the task?

4 25 workers were initially deployed to complete a construction project in 15 days. Three days after the project had started, they were informed that the project must be completed 2 days earlier than planned. How many more workers were then needed in order to meet the new requirement? (Assume that all the workers have the same work efficiency.)

10.16　Problem solving using four operations (2)

Learning objective

Solve problems using four operations

Basic questions

1 Think carefully and then draw a line to match each pair.

144 balloons are equally shared by six groups. Each group has four children. How many balloons will each child get on average?

(a) $144 \div (6 \times 4)$　　A. First find the number of balloons each group will get, and then divide it by 4 children in each group. The result is the number of balloons each child will get.

(b) $144 \div 6 \div 4$　　B. First find the total number of children in the six groups, and then divide the total number of balloons by the total number of children. The result is the number of balloons each child will get.

2 Please write two different number sentences with mixed operations and then calculate.

(a) A factory plans to produce 60 crystal balls per day with a target to produce 1620 crystal balls in total. The plan has been carried out for 9 days. How many more days are needed to meet the target?

Method 1:　　　　　　　　　　Method 2:

(b) Mrs. Lee made 56 toys in 4 hours. With this efficiency, how many toys can she make in one day if she works 8 hours a day?

Method 1:　　　　　　　　　　Method 2:

3 Application problems.

(a) A storybook has 460 pages. Lily read 120 pages in the first six days. At this pace, how many more days are needed for her to finish reading the whole book?

(b) A landscape company plans to complete the lawn treatment for the 82 800 square metres of lawns at a botanic garden in 60 working days. According to this plan, how many square metres of the lawns are still to be treated after 44 working days?

(c) A road construction team was repairing a 4920-metre road. They repaired 2400 metres in 20 days. At this efficiency level, after how many more days would the team finish the job?

(d) Four workers can produce 100 TV parts in five hours. At this efficiency level, how many workers are needed to produce 600 TV parts in 8 hours?

Challenge and extension questions

4 There is a five-digit number. The sum of any three neighbouring digits is 16. The digit in the ones place is 7 and that in the tens place is 3. What is the five-digit number?

5 A school bought 20 desks and 40 chairs at a total cost of £2400. The cost of one desk was equal to the cost of three chairs. How much did a desk and a chair cost respectively?

10.17　Problem solving using four operations (3)

Learning objective

Solve problems using four operations

Basic questions

1 A 'use your brain' shop never simply tells its customers the unit price of each item it sells. If you want to buy something, you are expected first to use your brain to think mathematically. The following table shows the information about the cost and quantity of purchase for some of the items it sells.

Items	Pencil	Eraser	Pen	Pencil-box
Quantity of purchase	8	3	5	10
Cost	£16	£12	£25	£270

(a) Aaron wants to buy 10 pencils, how much does he need to pay?

(b) Mr. Howard wants to buy pencil-boxes for 36 pupils, one pencil-box each person. How much does he need to pay?

(c) Ling wants to buy 2 erasers and 3 pens. How much does he need to pay?

(d) Mary's mother wants to buy 4 pencils and 2 erasers for Mary. How much does she need to pay?

2 Application problems.

(a) A company needed to assemble a batch of computers. 120 computers were assembled in the first 8 working days. At this rate, 24 more working days were needed to finish the job. How many computers did the company need to assemble?

(b) An arts and crafts manufacturer planned to produce 680 crafts items. It had produced 65 crafts items per day for the first 4 days. The remaining items needed to be produced in the next 6 days. How many items did it need to produce each day on average?

(c) A new highway is under construction. 240 km of it has been completed. The remaining part is 8 km longer than twice the completed part. What is the total length of the new highway?

(d) There are 150 apple trees in an orchard. There are 50 more pear trees than apple trees. The number of orange trees is 20 less than 3 times the number of pear trees. How many orange trees are there in the orchard?

Challenge and extension questions

3 When Ewa was doing an addition problem, she mistakenly read 0 in the ones place in one of the addends as 6 and the digit 2 in its tens place as 5. Therefore, her answer was 156. What is the correct answer?

4 Ben and his parents went orange picking in an orchard. They picked 78 oranges in total. Dad picked 11 more oranges than Mum. Ben picked 2 fewer oranges than Mum. How many oranges did each of them pick?

10.18 Problem solving using four operations (4)

Learning objective

Solve problems using four operations

Basic questions

1. Mrs. Chan went shopping with £200. She spent £137 on a set of English books. If she decided to use the money left to buy pens, costing £10 each, how many pens could she buy at most?

2. In a chicken farm, 160 eggs were laid in 8 minutes on its egg production line. Assuming the same rate, how many minutes would it take for 600 eggs to be laid?

3. 126 tiles of the same size have been used to floor 9 square metres. If 12 more square metres need to be floored, how many tiles are used altogether?

4. Three lorries of the same model can deliver 75 000 kg of goods in five trips. A supermarket needs 100 000 kg of goods to be delivered in two trips. How many such lorries does it need?

5. Jonathan borrowed a 255-page science book from his school library. He planned to finish reading the book in a week. He read 37 pages per day in the first five days. He wanted to read

the remaining pages over the weekend. How many pages did he still need to read each day?

6 A store has received a delivery of 900 kg of rice, which is in five sacks more than that of the flour it has received. Given that each sack of rice weighs 30 kg and each sack of flour weighs 25 kg, how many kilograms of flour has the store received?

7 A car can drive 60 km in 30 minutes. At this speed, how many kilometres can the car drive in seven hours?

8 A department store has received a delivery of 480 sweaters, which were packed in two plastic boxes and eight cardboard boxes. If the number of sweaters in two cardboard boxes is the same as the number of sweaters in one plastic box, how many sweaters are there in each plastic box and how many are in each cardboard box?

Challenge and extension questions

9 If six plates and three bowls cost £87, and two plates and three bowls cost £39, then how much does one plate cost? How much does one bowl cost?

10 Three children, A, B and C, have 108 pictures in total. Given that Child A has 18 fewer pictures than Child B, and Child C has 12 more pictures than Child B. How many pictures does each child have?

Unit test 10

1 Work these out mentally. Write the answers.

$24 \times 5 =$ $200 - 25 \times 4 =$ $125 \times (32 \div 4) =$

$450 \div 90 =$ $(90 - 60) \div 30 =$ $160 + 140 \div 70 =$

$4040 \div 40 =$ $(380 + 20) \times 2 =$ $25 \times 70 \times 4 =$

2 Use the column method to calculate. (Check the answer to the question marked with $*$.)

(a) $^* 615 \times 204 =$ (b) $5007 - 618 =$

3 Use your preferred methods to calculate, and show your working.

(a) $208 \times 13 - 6120 \div 30$ (b) $4 \times 505 \times 25$

(c) $[332 - (32 + 278)] \times 186$ (d) $30 \times (918 \div 9 + 18 \times 11)$

(e) $40 \times (250 \times 88)$ (f) 125×808

(g) $32 \times 64 - 23 \times 64 + 64$ (h) $(24 + 24 + 24) \times 25$

4 Fill in the brackets.

(a) In $175 \times 83 \times 4 = 83 \times (175 \times 4)$, the (   ) law of multiplication is used.

(b) In $\triangle + (56 + ☆) = (56 + ☆) + \triangle$, the (   ) law of addition is used.

(c) $◆ \times ★ + ● \times ★ = ($ _____ $+$ _____ $) \times ($ $)$

(d) $(33 + 16) + 84 = ($ $) + (16 +$ $)$

(e) $18 \times (27 + 5) = 18 \times ($ $) + ($ $) \times 5$

(f) $999 \times 78 + 78 \times ($ $) = 780\,000$

(g) A number is multiplied by 46 and 54 separately, and the sum of these two products is 4600. The number is (   ).

(h) A number is added to 5, then multiplied by 5, then again subtracted by 5, and finally divided by 5. The result is 5. The number is (   ).

(i) To calculate $100 - 52$ using the column method, 100 can be considered to consist of 9 tens and (   ) ones.

(j) A rope was 25 metres long. First (   ) metres were cut off and then another 3 metres were cut off. Afterwards the rope was 3 metres long.

(k) A number is divided by 8. Both the quotient and the remainder are 7. The number is (   ).

(l) When multiplying two numbers, Jim mistakenly read one of the factors 500 as 50 and got an answer of 450. The correct answer should be (   ).

(m) $650 - (210 - 40)$ is (   ) $650 - 210 - 40$. (Choose 'equal to' or 'greater than' or 'less than')

(n) work efficiency $= ($ $) \div ($ $)$.

5 True or false.

(a) $24 \times (68 + 32 \div 32 + 68) = 24 \times (100 \div 100) = 24 \times 1 = 24$

(   )

(b) $125 \times 24 = (125 \times 8) \times (125 \times 3)$ (   )

(c) In calculating $29 \times [3328 \div (32 \times 105 - 3328)]$ step by step, the second step is to find the difference between the product of 32 and 105 and 3328. ( )

(d) To find half of the difference between the product of 38 and 26 and 16, the number sentence is: $(38 \times 26 - 16) \div 2$. ( )

6 Write the number sentences and then calculate according to the following diagrams.

(a)

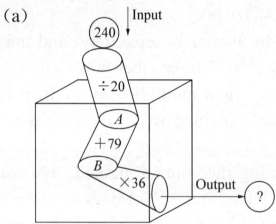

(b)

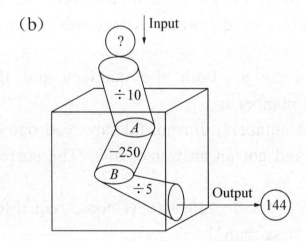

7 Write the number sentences and then calculate.

(a) After how many eighteens are taken away from 1100, is the result 2?

(b) The quotient of 840 divided by the difference of 129 and 59 is multiplied by 66. What is the product?

(c) A number is first subtracted by 3, then multiplied by 7, and finally added by 5. The result is 19. What is the number?

8 Application problems.

(a) The distance between Place A and Place B is 720 kilometres. A car has travelled 240 kilometres in three hours. At this speed, in how many hours will it reach Place B?

(b) A shipment of 120 containers of goods has reached a dock. It was supposed to unload 12 containers of the goods per hour. Due to an emergency, the shipment must be unloaded two hours ahead of the original plan. How many containers must be unloaded per hour now?

(c) A clothing manufacturer planned to make 60 sets of children's clothes, with each set using 110 cm of cloth. Later 100 cm of cloth was actually used for each set. How many more sets of children's clothing can be made with the same amount of cloth compared with the original plan?

(d) A store received a delivery of 1125 kg of pineapples. After 20 baskets of pineapples were sold there were 185 kg of pineapples remaining. If each basket came with the same weight, how many kilograms did each basket weigh?

End of year test

① Work these out mentally. Write the answers. （12%）

$9 \times 11 =$ $\qquad$ $500 \times 7 =$ $\qquad$ $12 \times 12 =$ $\qquad$ $20 + 20 \div 2 =$

$320 \div 4 \div 2 =$ $\qquad$ $1955 \div (\quad) = 5$ $\qquad$ $400 \div 4 + 20 \times 5 =$

$400 \times 15 =$ $\qquad$ $5087 \times 9 \times 0 =$ $\qquad$ $4250 - 50 + 3 \times 13 =$

$(80 \div 20 + 80) \div 4 =$ $\qquad$ $70 + (100 - 10 \times 5) =$

2 Use the column method to calculate. （Check the answer to the question marked with *.） （9%）

(a) $9485 - 4011 =$ $\qquad$ (b) $613 \times 64 =$ $\qquad$ (c) * $4902 + 2099 =$

❸ Work these out step by step. （Calculate smartly when possible.） （18%）

$(80 - 4) \times 125$ $\qquad$ $[138 - (15 \times 2 + 92)] \times 350$ $\qquad$ $32 \times 88 - 23 \times 88 + 88$

$\dfrac{2}{9} + \dfrac{3}{9} + \dfrac{4}{9} =$ $\qquad$ $\dfrac{17}{26} + \dfrac{9}{26} - \dfrac{3}{8} =$ $\qquad$ $1 - \dfrac{5}{7} - \dfrac{2}{7} =$

4 Write the number sentences and then calculate. (6%)

(a) A number is divided by 37. The quotient is 201 and the remainder is 17. What is this number?

(b) What is the number that is 36 less than 18 times 45?

5 Fill in the brackets. (13%)

(a) 48p＝(　　　) pounds

(b) 3 years and 9 months＝(　　　)months

(c) 25.35 km＝(　　　)km(　　　)m＝(　　　)m

(d) Put the five numbers 7999, 9908, 10,000, 8957, and 9889 in the order from the greatest to the smallest. The third number is (　　　).

(e) If $80.48 < 80.4\boxed{}$, the digit in the $\boxed{}$ should be (　　　).

(f) There are (　　　) 0.01s in 0.06.

(g) Using a fraction to express 0.91, it is (　　　).

(h) There are 45 children in a Year 4 class. If the number of boys is $\frac{4}{9}$ of the class, then the number of girls is (　　　).

(i) $0.204 = (\quad) \times \frac{1}{10} + (\quad) \times \frac{1}{100} + (\quad) \times 0.001$

(j) 18 identical squares can be put together to form (　　　) different rectangles.

(k) A triangle with (　　　) equal sides is called an equilateral triangle.

(l) If the side length of a square is increased so it is four times the original length, then the perimeter is (　　) times the original length and the area is (　　) times its original area.

(m) Write the Roman numerals in digits: LXVI=(　　); XCIV= (　　).

6 True or false. (5%)

(a) Triangles can be classified into acute-angled triangles, right-angled triangles and obtuse-angled triangles. (　　)

(b) A rectangle is a symmetrical figure. It has four lines of symmetry. (　　)

(c) The area of a square with side length of 0.1 m is 100 cm².

(　　)

(d) There are three dishes of non-vegetarian food and three dishes of vegetarian food. If everyone chooses one dish of vegetarian food and one dish of non-vegetarian food, there are six different selections. (　　)

(e) The result of 24×83 is between 1660 and 2490. It is nearer to 2490. (　　)

7 Multiple choice questions. (5%)

(a) The result of 125×24 is not equal to (　　).
A. 24×125
B. 125×20+4
C. 125×20+125×4
D. 125×8×3

(b) To simplify the decimal 90.060, (　　) zero(s) can be dropped off.
A. 1　　　　B. 2　　　　C. 3　　　　D. 0

(c) The number that has the same value as 3.06 is (　　).
A. 3.006　　B. 0.306　　C. 3.060　　D. 30 060

(d) The part of a line graph shown on the right generally represents (　　) over the period of time. 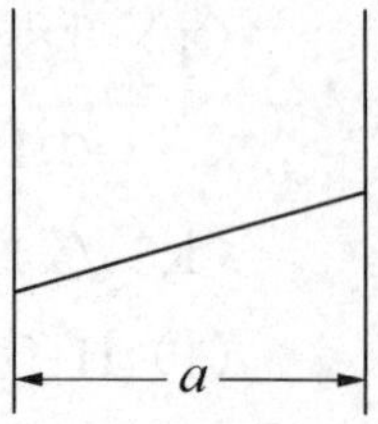
A. no change
B. upward trend

C. downward trend

D. trend uncertain

(e) The correct statement below is (   ).

A. Only squares and rectangles are quadrilaterals.

B. The longer the two sides of the angle, the greater the angle.

C. Squares are special quadrilaterals.

D. A triangle with acute angles is an acute-angled triangle.

8 Solve the following questions. (4%)

(a) Given the line of symmetry, draw the other half of the symmetrical figure below.

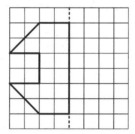

(b) Find the area of the following figure. (unit: cm; drawing not to scale.)

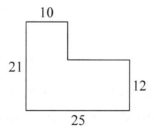

9 Application problems. (28%; 5 marks each for (a) to (d) and 8 marks for (e))

(a) 169 pupils of Year 3 are planning for an excursion. A bus can seat 30 pupils. How many buses do they need to hire so that everyone will have a seat?

(b) Lily is reading a book. She has read 36 pages. The number of unread pages is 18 times the number of pages she has read. How many pages does the book have?

(c) A school had a rectangular sports field 65 m long and 45 m wide. After expansion, the length increased by 10 m and the width increased by 5 m.
   (i) How many metres longer is the perimeter of the new sports field than that of the original one?

   (ii) How much larger is the area of the new sports field than that of the original one?

(d) A book is sold at £12.50. It will be £1.50 cheaper for each book if 10 or more books are bought. If buying 30 books or more, it will be £2 cheaper for each book. A school has bought 50 books. How much did it pay with the cheapest deal?

(e) The diagram below shows the number of rainy days each month in a particular year.

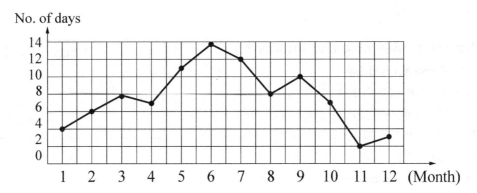

(i) It is a (   ) graph.

(ii) The most rainy month was (   ), and the least rainy month was (   ).

(iii) From the month of (   ) to (   ), the number of rainy days increased the most. From the month of (   ) to (   ) the number of rainy days decreased the most.

(iv) There were (   ) rainy days in total in that year.

Answers

Chapter 1 Revising and improving

1.1 Warm-up revision

1 500 230 500 600 240 60 1000 250 400 **2** 300 685 568 300 695 570 300 $875 - 170 = 705$ 572 $118 + 182 = 300$ 715 $220 + 354 = 574$

3 (a) 4 4 equal right 90 (b) 8 6 12 (c) 6 square **4** (a) kg hours minutes g (b) 1 77 120 458 52 2 366 **5** (a) 969 (b) 128 (c) 994

6 (a) $788 + 126 = 914$ (b) $593 - 384 = 209$ **7** (a) 10 180 (b) 20 6 120

8 6 6

1.2 Multiplication tables up to 12×12

1

×	1	2	3	4	5	6	7	8	9	10	11	12
10	10	20	30	40	50	60	70	80	90	100	110	120
11	11	22	33	44	55	66	77	88	99	110	121	132
12	12	24	36	48	60	72	84	96	108	120	132	144

2 $8 \times 11 = 88$, $11 \times 8 = 88$, $8 \times 11 = 88$, $10 \times 11 = 110$, $11 \times 10 = 110$, $10 \times 11 = 110$, $11 \times 12 = 132$, $12 \times 11 = 132$, $11 \times 12 = 132$ **3** 12 8 16, 11 4 22, 12 9 36 **4** 60 66 99 12, 55 77 144 3, 110 10 132 72 **5** $121 \div 11 = 11$ (bananas) **6** $11 \times 12 = 132$ (pages) $308 - 132 = 176$ (pages) **7** $11 \times 12 = 132$ (cards) **8** 26 or 136

1.3 Multiplication and division (1)

1 534 89 2848 1465 109 r 6 58
2 > > < < > < = > <
3 906 195 3829 **4** $36 \times 2 + 25 \times 2 = 122$ (pounds) **5** James runs the fastest John is the slowest

6

Number of pens									
£18	0	0	0	0	1	1	1	2	2	3
£9	0	2	4	6	0	2	4	0	2	0
£6	9	6	3	0	6	3	0	3	0	0

7 (a) $785 \times 9 = 7065$ (b) $822 \div 3 = 274$

1.4 Multiplication and division (2)

1 (a) 780 (b) 155 (c) 70 (d) 59 r 6
2 (a) 3601 (b) 2900 (c) 426
3 (a) $1000 \div 8 = 125$ (b) $721 \div 7 = 103$ (c) $5 \times 465 = 2325$ (d) $65 \times 8 + 9 = 529$ **4** (a) 1520 ml 2280 ml (b) 30 years (c) (i) 800 m (ii) 5 laps 200 m

5 10 footballs 30 basketballs **6** $125 \times 5 = 625$ $175 \times 5 = 875$

1.5 Problem solving (1)

1 159 books **2** 39 years old

3 (a) $34 + 34 \times 3 = 136$ $34 \times (3 + 1) = 136$ (b) $34 \times 3 - 34 = 68$ $34 \times (3 - 1) = 68$ **4** 96 stamps **5** (a) 1440 trees (b) 20 trees **6** 289 576

1.6 Problem solving (2)

1 (a) $32 + 32 \times 4 = 160$ (monkeys) (b) $19 \times 4 = 76$ (pencils) **2** (a) $357 \times 3 + 357 = 1428$ (b) $357 \div 3 + 357 = 476$ **3** 8000 kg
4 180 km **5** (a) 480 (b) 240 (c) 1080
6 42 pupils in the reading room, 30 pupils in the art room **7** 23 m

1.7 Fractions

1 $\frac{1}{2}$ $\frac{1}{8}$ $\frac{1}{4}$ **2** $\frac{2}{4}$ or $\frac{1}{2}$ $\frac{1}{3}$ $\frac{1}{4}$ $\frac{5}{6}$
3 2 wedges shaded, 1 triangle shaded, 2 parts shaded, 5 triangles shaded **4** circle

3◇ circle 6 △ ⑤ 10 4 15 ⑥ $\frac{1}{8}$

$\frac{1}{4}$ $\frac{2}{3}$ $\frac{2}{6}$ $\frac{1}{4}$ $\frac{2}{10}$ or $\frac{1}{5}$

Unit test 1

① (a) 600 (b) 360 (c) 90 (d) 144
(e) 2 (f) 4 (g) 4 (h) 10 (i) 132
(j) 50 (k) 80 (l) 10 ② (a) 112
(b) 321 (c) 855 (d) 180 (e) 12 r 5
(f) 40 r 5 ③ (a) 172 (b) 257 (c) 573
(d) 7800 (e) 16 (f) 453 ④ (a) 864
(b) 50, 700, 240 (c) < > < >
> < (d) cm g cm kg m pounds
m cm km (e) $\frac{1}{6}$ (f) 9 (g) $\frac{23}{34}$
(h) 3 (i) $\frac{1}{5}$ m $\frac{4}{5}$ ⑤ two wedges
shaded, five parts shaded, one triangle
shaded ⑥ $\frac{1}{4}$ $\frac{2}{8}$, $\frac{1}{4}$ $\frac{3}{12}$, $\frac{1}{2}$ $\frac{4}{8}$
⑦ (a) 4 cuts (b) 36 metres (c) 60 metres
(d) 67 words (e) (i) £182 (ii) £54
(iii) £164

Chapter 2 Numbers to and beyond 1000 and their calculation

2.1 Knowing numbers beyond 1000 (1)

① 174 24 6 36 112 3 4 0 63 6
174 27 ② (b) one thousand three
hundred and forty-four 1000 300 40 4
(c) five thousand five hundred and eighty-
six 5000 500 80 6 (d) six thousand
seven hundred 6000 700 0 0 (e) six
thousand eight hundred and fifty-three
6000 800 50 3 ③

Ten thousands	Thousands	Hundreds	Tens	Ones
0	1	0	0	1

Ten thousands	Thousands	Hundreds	Tens	Ones
0	9	2	1	2

Ten thousands	Thousands	Hundreds	Tens	Ones
0	7	0	3	5

Ten thousands	Thousands	Hundreds	Tens	Ones
1	0	5	3	5

④ (a) 4 0 (b) 50 500 5000 (c) ones
tens (d) thousands hundreds ten thousands
(e) thousands 7 ones four thousand
and seventy-five 3076 ⑤ (a) B (b) C
(c) B (d) C ⑥ 2000 1100 1010
1001 ⑦ answer may vary

2.2 Knowing numbers beyond 1000 (2)

① (a) 4 5 6 8 9 10 (b) 40 50
60 80 90 100 (c) 400 500 600 800
900 1000 (d) 4000 5000 6000 8000
9000 10 000 (e) 100 125 150 200
225 250 ② (a) 1737 1739, 9998
10 000, 4105 4107, 5999 6001 (b) 3890
3910, 1540 1560, 7799 7819, 5990
6010 (c) 2557 2757, 4405 4605, 7690
7890, 5900 6100 (d) 67 2067, 8222
10 222, 3050 5050, 5000 7000
③ (a) 237 238 (b) 1075 1100
(c) 6500 8500 (d) 6000 5000 (e) 2000
1500 1000 500 0 ④ (a) 3280 4990
5010 (b) 6000 (c) 1000 6000 (d) 8880
6540 6000 5010 4990 3280 1000
⑤ 2036 8632 ⑥ 1300 301 300

2.3 Rounding numbers to the nearest 10, 100 and 1000

① A = 3700 B = 4200 C = 5900 D =
7100 E = 8000 F = 8500 ② numbers
correctly marked on the number line
③ (a) A D E (b) B C F ④ (a) √
(b) × (c) × (d) √ (e) √ (f) √
⑤ (a) 40 10 90 500 200 2020

4090 10 000 (b) 100 300 1000 1500
3000 5100 8100 10 000 (c) 0 0 1000
2000 5000 7000 8000 10 000 ⑥ 45
46 47 48 49 ⑦ 6995 6996 6997
6998 6999 7001 7002 7003 7004

2.4 Addition with four-digit numbers (1)

① (a) 7346 3175 (b) 8586 7768
(c) 5533 4598 (d) 7642 9001
② 13 257 6664 9878 ③ answers may
vary ④ (a) $1554 + 1000 = 2554$
(b) $5528 - 1000 = 4528$ (c) $2139 + 3324 = 5463$ ⑤ (a) four (b) five
(c) five four

2.5 Addition with four-digit numbers (2)

① (a) 4734 (b) 7431 (c) 7320
(d) 6087 (e) 8716 ② 2477 5532 4849
8611 5722 10 000 ③ (a) ✕ 4004
(b) ✕ 9152 (c) ✕ 1506 ④ (a) 57 279
(b) 14 333 ⑤ (a) 2500 m (b) £5460
(c) 5865 kilowatts ⑥ $3922 + 3833 = 7755$ $96 + 2622 = 2718$ $5378 + 27 922 = 33 300$

2.6 Subtractions with four-digit numbers (1)

① (a) 2242 4303 (b) 2653 3601
(c) 3021 4509 (d) 5381 5439 ② (a) 3434
(b) 2831 (c) 1093 (d) 3295 (e) 2165
(f) 5573 ③ answers may vary
④ (a) $5032 - 3415 = 1617$ (b) $9418 - 2280 = 7138$ ⑤ (a) $9550 - 7450 = 2100$
(grams) (b) $7450 - 2100 = 5350$ (grams)

2.7 Subtraction with four-digit numbers (2)

① (a) 3232 (b) 2371 (c) 872 (d) 4168
(e) 2139 (f) 5987 ② (a) ✕ 2346
(b) ✕ 3291 (c) ✕ 609 ③ 7204
4296 2181 136 3178 439
④ (a) $7597 - 4059 = 3538$ (b) $8400 - 7195 = 1205$ (c) $6783 - 435 = 6348$
⑤ (a) 22 062 (b) 2509 ⑥ (a) 7803 km
(b) The flight to Beijing on the second day
was longer. It was longer by 2575 km. The
total distance he flew in the two days was
13 747 km. ⑦ (a) 9 (b) 8

2.8 Estimating and checking answers using inverse operations

① 6000 2200 8700 8800 5200 900

6700 220 800 3100 2000 9020 ②

	2132	5522	4590	6705	1848	8999
Nearest 10	2130	5520	4590	6710	1850	9000
Nearest 100	2100	5500	4600	6700	1800	9000
Nearest 1000	2000	6000	5000	7000	2000	9000

③ 3700 3701, 8000 8740, 9900 9877,
3400 3356, 300 326, 10 000 10 025
④ 5000 5425, 10 000 9986, 9000
9768, 2000 2211, 4000 3634, 9000 8458
⑤ (b) No. It is $5548 + 4371 = 9919$ $9919 - 5548 = 4371$ (c) No. It is $9208 - 3257 = 5951$ $5951 + 3257 = 9208$ or $9208 - 5951 = 3257$ (d) No. It is $8399 + 699 = 9098$
$9098 - 699 = 8399$ or $9098 - 8399 = 699$
(e) $2391 + 1641 = 4032$. Yes, it checks.
(f) No. It is $10 000 - 4075 = 5925$ $5925 + 4075 = 10 000$ or $10 000 - 5925 = 4075$
⑥ (a) 3475 litres 6985 litres (b) (i)
No, it is not sufficient. (ii) £600 more is
needed to purchase the two items.
⑦ (a) 2688 or 2868 or 2886 (b) 6288

Unit test 2

① 5000 8000 9990 7000 3000 3060
90 3000 8220 ② A = 1700 B =
2200 C = 3900 D = 5100 E = 6000
F = 6500 ③ (a) 520 525 (b) 805
905 (c) 8000 9000 (d) 125 100
(e) 48 60 72 ④

Thousands	Hundreds	Tens	Ones
3	0	1	9

Thousands	Hundreds	Tens	Ones
7	9	0	9

Thousands	Hundreds	Tens	Ones
1	5	3	5

Thousands	Hundreds	Tens	Ones
1	0	0	0

⑤ (a) 6750 (b) 1083 (c) 8200 (d) 2651

(e) 3089 **6** 6000 5888, 6000 6488, 6000 5216, 4000 4491 **7** (a) 10 000 − 1000 = 9000 (b) 8569 − 3378 = 5191 (c) 8288 + 3009 = 11 297 **8** (a) £17 608 (b) £1508 **9** 3726 pupils **10** (a) The flight from Rome to London on the first day is longer. It is longer by 277 km. (b) 2591 km

Chapter 3 Multiplying by a two-digit number

3.1 Multiplying whole tens by a two-digit number

1 (a)

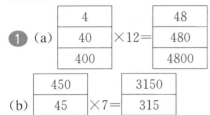

(c) 48 480 (d) 315 3150 (e) 48 4800 (f) 315 31 500 **2** 22 45 270 220 450 2700 2200 4500 27 000 2200 4500 27 000 **3** 3780 3000 1000 340 1260 900 2250 1440 9000 100 2640 11 900 6500 3200 660 32 400 **4** = > > < **5** (a) 204 180 24 204 (b) 364 350 14 364 **6** (a) × (b) √ (c) √ (d) √ √ **7** (b) 3200 (c) 37 200 (d) 9800 **8** (a) $12 \times 60 = 720$ (b) $800 \times 25 = 20\,000$ **9** Method 1: $24 \times 50 + 24 \times 70 = 2880$ (pence) Method 2: $24 \times (50 + 70) = 2880$ (pence) **10** (b) 60 (c) 50

3.2 Multiplying a two-digit number by a two-digit number (1)

1 (a) 160 (b) 80 (c) 240 (d) 25 (e) 240 (f) 120 (g) 360 (h) 15 (i) 330 (j) 165 (k) 495 (l) 15 **2** (a) 300 360 260 52 312 (b) 1800 2000 1860 62 1922 **3** $48 \times 25 = 12 \times 4 \times 25 = 12 \times 100 = 1200$; $48 \times 25 = 40 \times 25 + 8 \times 25 = 1000 + 200 = 1200$; $48 \times 25 = 50 \times 25 − 2 \times 25 = 1250 + 50 = 1200$ **4** $19 \times 21 =$ $19 \times 20 + 19 \times 1 = 380 + 19 = 399$; $33 \times 77 = 33 \times 70 + 33 \times 7 = 2310 + 231 = 2541$; $51 \times 63 = 50 \times 63 + 1 \times 63 = 3150 + 63 = 3213$ (answer may vary) **5** (a) $11 \times 55 = 605$ (b) $550 − 19 \times 19 = 189$ **6** A = 4 B = 2 C = 8 D = 5 E = 7

3.3 Multiplying a two-digit number by a two-digit number (2)

1 315 371 160 150 1052 3 42 000 19 880 2000 660 750 **2** 3120 240 5 288 6 3120 **3** 286 7425 3024 **4** (a) In the column calculation, 44×50 is 2200, not 220; the correct answer is 2420. (b) 37×10 is 370, not 37; the correct answer is 444. (c) 26×90 is 2340, not 234; the correct answer is 2548. **5** (a) $89 \times 89 = 7921$ (b) $99 \times 99 = 9801$ **6** (a) $99 \times 33 + 99 = 3300$ (pounds) (b) $2 \times 53 \times 2 = 212$ (pupils) **7** 121 121 144 132 169 143 196 154 225 165 256 176 289 187 324 198 361 209

3.4 Multiplying a three-digit number by a two-digit number (1)

1 375 625 875 500 325 625 750 1125 500 750 1000 1375 **2** (a) 4000 6000 4480 672 5152 (b) 4600 6900 4580 229 4809 **3** 27 170 2090 2508 27 170 **4** 5 4 357 9 357 8 **5** 3597 8192 54 945 **6** (a) $222 \times 55 = 12\,210$ (b) $99 \times 999 = 98\,901$ **7** $329 + (329 \times 12 − 300) = 3977$ (pounds) **8** (a) 150 seconds (b) 514

3.5 Multiplying a three-digit number by a two-digit number (2)

1 28 30 39 280 300 390 2800 30 000 39 000 **2** 520 130 182 000 000 **3** (b) 100 880 100 88 000 (c) 10 6720 10 67 200 **4** (b) 45 000 (c) 3200 (d) 32 000 **5** (a) A (b) D (c) C (d) A **6** (a) 19 893 (b) 13 376 (c) 630 000 (d) 8112 (e) 19 162 (f) 35 552 **7** (a) $200 \times 12 \times 12 = 28\,800$ (b) $160 \times 50 + 50 = 8050$ **8** $32 \times 20 = 640$ (pupils), $1000 > 640$, Yes. $1000 − 640 = 360$ (seats)

3.6 Dividing two-digit or three-digit numbers by tens

1 40 30 120 70 4 3 12 7 **2** 3
7 5 9 6 4 **3** (b) 9 9 9 2 9 2
(c) 3 4 3 3 3 15 (d) 8 9 8 8 8
16 **4** (b) 7 r 5 (c) 7 r 12 (d) 5 r 10
(e) 9 r 5 (f) 7 r 36 **5** (a) $292 \div 60 = 4$
r 52 (b) $99 \div 20 = 4$ r 19 **6**

Rows	10	20	30	40	60	80
Number of pupils in each row	72	36	24	18	12	9

7 (a) 80 (b) Alvin Peter (c) 66
(d) 5

3.7 Practice and exercise

1 480 17 0 240 340 105 1010 8
2 6237 10 016 852 600 85 r 1 (85 ×
30 + 1 = 2551) **3** 7810 640 324 10
4 (a) $480 + 480 \div 6 = 560$ (b) $(565 +$
$19) \div 50 = 11$ r 34 **5** (a) $25 \times 30 + 25 \times$
$6 = 900$, $20 \times 36 + 5 \times 36 = 900$, $25 \times$
$6 \times 6 = 900$ (b) 5 (c) 35 (d) 10 120
10 12 (e) 4 **6** (a) 120 (b) 6000
7 $300 \div 5 = 60$ (trees)

Unit test 3

1 500 3330 47 r 10 10 9600 1000
50 70 375 11 1250 6 **2** (a) 8901
(b) 2 024 000 (c) 9840 (d) 19 552
(e) 141 r 26 (f) 338 r 19 **3** (a) 2254
(b) 3130 (c) 4500 (d) 1818 (e) 30
(f) 2925 **4** (a) 4 (b) 1099 (c) three
hundreds 2 (d) 6 1−5 (e) 4
5 (a) D (b) C (c) C (d) B
6 (a) $10 \times 12 \times 12 = 1440$ (eggs) $1440 \div$
$80 = 18$ (days) (b) $3680 \times 3 = 11\,040$ (kg)
(c) $(730 + 350) \div 20 = 54$ (tons) (d) $10 -$
$200 \div 100 = 8$ (pounds) $85 - 500 \div 100 =$
80 (pounds)

Chapter 4 Addition and subtraction of fractions

4.1 Fractions in hundredths

1 (a) $\frac{1}{2}$ (b) $\frac{3}{10}$ (c) $\frac{1}{100}$ (d) $\frac{3}{200}$

(e) $\frac{7}{800}$ **2** (b) 10 squares shaded
(c) 1 square shaded (d) 89 squares shaded
3 lines drawn from $\frac{1}{3}$ to $\frac{9}{27}$ to $\frac{10}{30}$, $\frac{9}{10}$ to
$\frac{90}{100}$ to $\frac{18}{20}$, $\frac{2}{5}$ to $\frac{40}{100}$ to $\frac{80}{200}$ **4** fractions
correctly marked on the number lines.
5 (a) $\frac{7}{100}$ $\frac{9}{100}$ $\frac{11}{100}$ $\frac{13}{100}$ (b) $\frac{41}{100}$
$\frac{51}{100}$ $\frac{61}{100}$ $\frac{71}{100}$ (c) $\frac{85}{100}$ $\frac{81}{100}$
$\frac{77}{100}$ $\frac{73}{100}$ **6** (a) $\frac{20}{200}$ (b) $\frac{38}{200}$ (c) $\frac{60}{200}$
(d) $\frac{42}{200}$ (e) $\frac{40}{200}$ **7** (a) $\frac{1}{100}$ (b) 50 5

4.2 Addition and subtraction of fractions (1)

1 (a) 7 3 4 7 $\frac{7}{10}$ $\frac{7}{10}$ (b) 16 7
9 16 $\frac{16}{17}$ (c) adding up unchanged
2 (a) $\frac{4}{7}$ (b) $\frac{3}{5}$ (c) $\frac{13}{20}$ (d) $\frac{22}{43}$
(e) $\frac{60}{77}$ (f) $\frac{460}{800}$ (g) $\frac{8}{9}$ (h) $\frac{26}{32}$
3 (a) 13 $\frac{8}{9}$ (b) $\frac{5}{6}$ 1 (c) $\frac{5}{12}$
4 (a) $\frac{5}{20} + \frac{7}{20} = \frac{12}{20}$ (b) $\frac{11}{19} + \frac{3}{19} = \frac{14}{19}$
5 $\frac{9}{10}$ **6** (a) $\frac{2}{10}$ (b) $\frac{7}{10}$ (c) $\frac{2}{22}$
(d) 40 6 **7** $\frac{1}{6} + \frac{1}{30}$ $\frac{1}{10} + \frac{1}{90}$ $\frac{1}{51} + \frac{1}{2550}$

4.3 Addition and subtraction of fractions (2)

1 (a) 6 9 3 6 $\frac{6}{10}$ $\frac{6}{10}$ (b) 7 16
9 $\frac{7}{17}$ (c) subtracting unchanged
2 (a) $\frac{1}{6}$ (b) $\frac{6}{14}$ (c) $\frac{9}{30}$ (d) $\frac{13}{72}$
(e) $\frac{50}{300}$ (f) $\frac{2}{25}$ (g) $\frac{38}{65}$ (h) 21 (i) 7
3 (a) $\frac{11}{15} + \frac{3}{15} = \frac{14}{15}$ (b) $\frac{8}{20} - \frac{4}{20} = \frac{4}{20}$
(c) $\frac{7}{7} - \frac{3}{7} = \frac{4}{7}$ **4** (a) $\frac{1}{10}$ (b) $\frac{9}{10}$
(c) 2 (d) $\frac{5}{8}$ **5** No, there were no

more pieces left for Dad. (Hint: $\frac{3}{4}$ equals $\frac{6}{8}$, 2 units of $\frac{1}{8}$ equals $\frac{2}{8}$, $\frac{6}{8} + \frac{2}{8} = 1$)

4. 4 Fun with exploration – 'fraction wall'

1 answer may vary **2** (a) $<$ (b) $>$ (c) $<$ (d) $=$ (e) $<$ (f) $>$ **3** (a) 1 (b) $\frac{2}{12}$ (c) $\frac{6}{7}$ **4** (a) $\frac{2}{3}$, $\frac{6}{9}$, $\frac{8}{12}$ (b) $\frac{4}{6}$, $\frac{6}{9}$, $\frac{8}{12}$ (c) $\frac{6}{8}$, $\frac{9}{12}$, $\frac{12}{16}$ (d) $\frac{2}{8}$, $\frac{3}{12}$, $\frac{4}{16}$ **5** $\frac{1}{16}$

Unit test 4

1 (a) 84 (b) 63 (c) 36 (d) 320 (e) 500 (f) 82 (g) $\frac{3}{7}$ (h) $\frac{23}{23}$ or 1 (i) $\frac{8}{16}$ (j) $\frac{6}{13}$ (k) $\frac{3}{5}$ (l) $\frac{11}{16}$ **2** (a) $\frac{6}{8}$ (b) $\frac{2}{11}$ (c) $\frac{4}{14}$ (d) $\frac{17}{25}$ (e) $\frac{43}{74}$ (f) $\frac{4}{14}$ **3** (a) 30 squares shaded (b) 77 squares shaded **4** (a) 6 32 (b) 2 20 (c) 5 (d) $\frac{50}{100}$ or $\frac{1}{2}$ (e) 7 $\frac{1}{11}$ (f) $\frac{1}{100}$ (g) 5 4 **5** (a) C (b) B **6** (a) $\frac{4}{5} - \frac{1}{5} = \frac{3}{5}$ (b) $\frac{79}{80} - \frac{50}{80} + \frac{30}{80} = \frac{59}{80}$ **7** (a) $1200 \times 4 \times 2 = 9600$ (books) (b) $\frac{5}{22}$ (c) 750 g

Chapter 5 Consolidation and enhancement

5.1 Multiplication and multiplication table

1

×	1	2	3	4	5	6	7	8	9	10	11	12
1	1	2	3	4	5	6	7	8	9	10	11	12
2	2	4	6	8	10	12	14	16	18	20	22	24
3	3	6	9	12	15	18	21	24	27	30	33	36
4	4	8	12	16	20	24	28	32	36	40	44	48
5	5	10	15	20	25	30	35	40	45	50	55	60
6	6	12	18	24	30	36	42	48	54	60	66	72
7	7	14	21	28	35	42	49	56	63	70	77	84
8	8	16	24	32	40	48	56	64	72	80	88	96
9	9	18	27	36	45	54	63	72	81	90	99	108
10	10	20	30	40	50	60	70	80	90	100	110	120
11	11	22	33	44	55	66	77	88	99	110	121	132
12	12	24	36	48	60	72	84	96	108	120	132	144

2 (a) 56 $7 \times 8 = 56$ $8 \times 7 = 56$ $56 \div 7 = 8$ $56 \div 8 = 7$ (b) 88, $8 \times 11 = 88$ $11 \times 8 = 88$ $88 \div 8 = 11$ $88 \div 11 = 8$ (c) 60 $5 \times 12 = 60$ $12 \times 5 = 60$ $60 \div 5 = 12$ $60 \div 12 = 5$ (d) 10 $6 \times 10 = 60$ $10 \times 6 = 60$ $60 \div 6 = 10$ $60 \div 10 = 6$ (e) 8 $8 \times 9 = 72$ $9 \times 8 = 72$ $72 \div 8 = 9$ $72 \div 9 = 8$ (f) 11 $11 \times 12 = 132$ $12 \times 11 = 132$ $132 \div 11 = 12$ $132 \div 12 = 11$ **3** (a) 4 3 12 (b) 9 6 54 (c) 6 11 66 (d) 5 7 35 (e) 8 12 96 **4** $40 \times 2 = 80$ $40 \times 3 = 120$ **5** (a) 12 outfits (b) 20 combinations **6** 12 ways **7** 400 ways

5. 2 Relationship between addition and subtraction

1 (a) (i) 130 50 50 (ii) 100 53 53 47 (iii) 160 160 230 (iv) 100 100 190 90 (b) Sum Difference Difference Minuend Addition **2** (a) $-$ $-$ (b) $-$ $+$ (c) $868 - 756$ $868 - 112$ (d) $\bigcirc + \triangle$ $\square - \triangle$ **3** (b) 235 (c) 101 (d) 265 **4** (a) $789 - 126 = 663$ (b) $120 - 60 = 60$ **5** (a) $\times$ (b) $\checkmark$ **6** $278 - 63 = 215$

5. 3 Relationship between multiplication and division

1 (a) (i) 110 22 22 (ii) 12 120 12 (iii) 1000 8 125 (v) 140 35 35 (b) Product Dividend Quotient (c) dividend ($\checkmark$) **2** (b) 12 (c) 108 (d) 15 (e) 9 (f) 2760 **3** (a) $768 \div 8 = 96$ (b) $(288 - 4) \div 2 = 142$ (c) $840 \div 30 = 28$ **4** $360 \div 30 \times 32 = 384$ **5** divisor: $210 \div (9 + 1) = 21$ dividend: $210 - 21 = 189$

5. 4 Multiplication by two-digit numbers

1 880 45 750 30 90 2040 2 20 360 20 168 16 **2** (a) 6048 (b) 87 (c) 16 200 **3** $82 \times 54 = 4428$ $25 \times 48 = 1200$ **4** $(25 + 19) \times 12 = 528$ (pounds) **5** $(9720 - 90 \times 12) = 8640$ (pounds) **6** (a) 900 60 (b) four 840 1260

1260 (c) four ⑦

$$\begin{array}{r} 1\ 7 \\ \times\ \ 6\ 4 \\ \hline 6\ 8 \\ 1\ 0\ 2 \\ \hline 1\ 0\ 8\ 8 \end{array}$$

5.5 Practice with fractions

① $\frac{2}{8}$ or $\frac{1}{4}$ $\frac{4}{8}$ or $\frac{1}{2}$ $\frac{6}{12}$ or $\frac{1}{2}$ ② 3

squares shaded 4 squares shaded 5

squares shaded ③ (a) $\frac{1}{12}$ (b) 6 (c) $\frac{17}{23}$

(d) $\frac{5}{6}$ $\frac{8}{9}$ (e) 7 (f) 4 (g) 2 (h) 9 8

(i) infinitely many (j) 5 ④ (a) $\frac{3}{4}$

(b) $\frac{68}{250}$ (c) $\frac{12}{50}$ (d) $\frac{6}{7}$ ⑤ $\frac{99}{100}$, $\frac{1}{2}$

$\frac{49}{100}$, $\frac{1}{10}$, $\frac{1}{100}$ ⑥ (a) $\frac{1}{8}$ $\frac{1}{8}$ $\frac{5}{8}$ (b) 5

(c) $\frac{18}{20}$ (d) 4 18 27 8 16

5.6 Roman numerals to 100

① 11:52 a.m. or 11:52 p.m., 2:48 a.m. or 2:48 p.m., 9:30 a.m. or 9:30 p.m. ②

I	II	III	IV	V	VI	VII	VIII	IX	X
XI	XII	XIII	XIV	XV	XVI	XVII	XVIII	XIX	XX
XXI	XXII	XXIII	XXIV	XXV	XXVI	XXVII	XXVIII	XXIX	XXX
XXXI	XXXII	XXXIII	XXXIV	XXXV	XXXVI	XXXVII	XXXVIII	XXXIX	XL
XLI	XLII	XLIII	XLIV	XLV	XLVI	XLVII	XLVIII	XLIX	L
LI	LII	LIII	LIV	LV	LVI	LVII	LVIII	LIX	LX
LXI	LXII	LXIII	LXIV	LXV	LXVI	LXVII	LXVIII	LXIX	LXX
LXXI	LXXII	LXXIII	LXXIV	LXXV	LXXVI	LXXVII	LXXVIII	LXXIX	LXXX
LXXXI	LXXXII	LXXXIII	LXXXIV	LXXXV	LXXXVI	LXXXVII	LXXXVIII	LXXXIX	XC
XCI	XCII	XCIII	XCIV	XCV	XCVI	XCVII	XCVIII	XCIX	C

③ lines drawn from V to 5, L to 50, I to 1, X to 10 and C to 100. ④ XLIII LV XII XCVIII LXXVII LX IX LXXXIV ⑤ 6 52 79 9 95 65 19 70 ⑥ (a) first chapter: 24 pages second chapter: 30 pages third chapter: 6 pages (b) 60 ⑦ (a) √ (b) × (c) √

Unit test 5

① (a) 57 (b) 130 (c) 180 (d) 440 (e) 720 (f) 75 (g) 13 (h) 30 (i) 32
② (a) 7307 (b) 739 (c) 9 (d) 55 (e) 1339 (f) 2 ③ (a) 3978 (b) 26 180 (c) 27 ④ (a) 429 (b) 3600 (c) 37 (d) 310 ⑤ (a) 0 (b) $\frac{24}{35}$ (c) $\frac{2}{9}$ ⑥ 6 14 97 42 55 79 ⑦ (a) inverse

subtrahend difference minuend (b) 32 (c) 3760 (d) 9000 (e) 4 (f) 4 5
⑧ (a) $220-96=124$ (b) $(5\times8)\div4=10$ (c) $(408+65)\times2=946$ ⑨ (a) $42\times5 = 210$ (pages) (b) $100-38-53 = 9$ (years old) $100-38 = 62$ (years old)
(c) $98\times6+606 = 1194$ (pounds) (d) $36-36\div4 = 27$ (balls) (e) $288-(69-4) = 223$
(f) 6 combinations

Chapter 6 Introduction to decimals
6.1 Decimals in life
① (a) 112.7 1.8 12.75 2.72 (b) 105 106 106 112 113 113 (c) 1 2 2 (d) 12 13 13 (e) 2 3 3 ② (a) 13 20 thirteen point two zero (b) 7 0 seven

point zero zero　(c) 21　68　twenty-one point six eight　**3**　1. 25 m or 1. 52 m 34. 5 kg or 35. 4 kg or 43. 5 kg or 45. 3 kg or 53. 4 kg or 54. 3 kg

6. 2　Understanding decimals (1)

1　(a) $\frac{1}{10}$　$\frac{9}{10}$　whole (b) $\frac{3}{10}$　$\frac{4}{10}$　$\frac{3}{10}$

(c) $<$　$>$　$=$　(d) 0.1　0.2　$\frac{3}{10}$

(e) decimals　0.1　zero point one　0.01 zero point zero one　0.001　zero point zero zero one　**2** 0.25　0.5　0.75

3 (a) 0. 7　zero point seven　(b) 0. 16 zero point one six　(c) 0. 256　zero point two five six　(d) 0. 8　zero point eight (e) 0. 205　zero point two zero five

(f) 0. 95　zero point nine five　**4**　(a) $\frac{5}{10}$

(b) $\frac{3}{100}$　(c) $\frac{24}{100}$　(d) $\frac{1}{1000}$　(e) $\frac{207}{1000}$

(f) $\frac{9}{10}$　**5**　(b) $\frac{62}{100}$　0. 62　zero point six

two　(c) $\frac{275}{1000}$　0. 275　zero point two

seven five　(d) $\frac{30}{100}$　0. 30 or 0. 3　zero point three zero or zero point three

6 Simon　$200 \div 10 \times 4 = 80$ (ml)　$200 \div 10 \times 5 = 100$ (ml)　**7** 12

6. 3　Understanding decimals (2)

1 See table below

Whole number part				Decimal point	Decimal part		
Thousands place	Hundreds place	Tens place	Ones place	•	Tenths place	Hundredths place	Thousandths place
6	7	3	5	•	4	8	2

2 (a) 0. 4　0. 5　0. 6　0. 7　0. 8　0. 9 (b) 5. 14　5. 15　5. 16　5. 17　5. 18　5. 19 (c) 8　7.5　7　6.5　6　5.5　**3** (a) 0. 4 0. 7　0. 9　(b) 1　(c) 1　1　(d) 10　100 1000　(e) 10　10　**4** (a) whole number decimal　(b) 6　7　(c) 0. 2　0. 05　0. 128 (d) tens　ones　tenth　hundredths　thousandths (e) ones　ones　tenths　one　hundredths hundredths　**5**　(a) A　(b) B　(c) C (d) D　**6**　(a) 0. 065　(b) 601. 03 (c) 400. 004　**7** 93. 1 to 93. 9 (answer may vary)

6. 4　Understanding decimals (3)

1　(a) 2040. 1　(b) 1. 43　(c) 15. 045 (d) mixed decimals: 5. 11　3. 03,　pure decimals: 0. 41　0. 8　(e) 0. 12　0. 21 **2** (b) 4　4　8　(c) 8　2　5　7　(d) 0. 1 0. 01　**3** (a) ×　(b) √　(c) ×　(d) × (e) √　(f) ×　(g) √　**4**　(a) 639. 18 (b) 200　(c) 0. 126　0. 621　10. 26 (d) 100　1　10　(e) 0. 9　1. 01　(f) one hundred

6. 5　Understanding decimals (4)

1　(a) ten point seven nine　(b) twenty two point zero two three　(c) nine point three zero four　(d) zero point zero one zero one　(e) fourteen point nine zero (f) three hundred point three zero three (g) 0. 17　(h) 60. 98　(i) 20. 002　(j) 100. 375 (k) 0. 8060　(l) 100. 900　**2** 0. 9, 24. 8, 80. 9, 100. 9　54. 32, 0. 31, 46. 73, 0. 18, 9. 45, 5. 77, 0. 07　12. 976, 1. 244, 7. 201 **3** (a) 9　0. 1　0. 9　(b) 99　0. 01　0. 99 (c) 999　0. 001　0. 999　(d) 0. 94　0. 96 (e) two　hundredths　4 hundredths　tens 4 tens　1000　**4** answers may vary

5 $\frac{112}{100}$　$1\frac{12}{100}$　$\frac{5833}{100}$　$58\frac{33}{100}$　**6** 99. 09

6. 6　Understanding decimals (5)

1 1. 7　4. 4　3　0. 01　0. 03　$\frac{3}{100}$

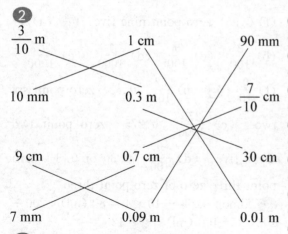

$\frac{3}{10}$ m   1 cm   90 mm

10 mm   0.3 m $\frac{7}{10}$ cm

9 cm   0.7 cm   30 cm

7 mm   0.09 m   0.01 m

3 (a) 2.1 cm 1 cm (b) 0.13 cm
4 sides correctly measured and added to get the perimeter **5** (530 + 50) × 2 = 1160 (ml) **6** (a) $\frac{6}{10}$ 0.6 $\frac{8}{1000}$ 0.008
(b) 3004.0908 (c) 1.1 (d) 0.25

6.7 Understanding decimals (6)

1 (a) 8 721 (b) 20.220 (c) 215.95
(d) 1020.061 (e) 8.03 (f) 1000 (g) 2793
(h) 400.004 mixed (i) zero point seven zero seven pure (j) 9 **2** (a) C A D
B (b) C (c) B (d) C (e) C (f) C B
A **3** 96.829

6.8 Comparing decimals (1)

1 (a) numbers correctly marked on the number line (b) 7.7 0.4 (c) Yes, the further the numbers away from the original point, the greater the number is (d) 7.7 > 5.8 > 4.5 > 2.1 > 0.4 **2** whole number greater tenths tenths **3** (a) >
(b) > (c) < (d) < (e) < (f) >
4 (a) 9.09 > 0.99 > 0.909 > 0.9
(b) 22.202 > 22.20 > 22.02 > 22.002
5 John is the tallest. Mathew is the heaviest. **6** Eileen **7** 0 0 6 − 9
8 0.24 < 0.26 < 0.42 < 0.46 < 0.62 < 0.64

6.9 Comparing decimals (2)

1 (a) > (b) > (c) < (d) < (e) >
(f) > **2** (a) 2 (b) 5 (c) 5 (d) 8
(e) 10 (f) 3 (g) 5 5 **3** lines drawn from 1.6 to 2, 212.9 to 213, 1.9 to 2, 213.1 to 213, 0.3 to 0, 2.5 to 3. **4** (a) 2 m < 2.04 m < 2.4 m < 2.44 m (b) 0.58 kg <

0.59 kg < 5.8 kg < 5.9 kg **5** Joan
6 11 35 15 7 111 1000
7 Person A: 21.5 kg Person B: 21.46 kg
Person C: 21.52 kg Person D: 21.38 kg

6.10 Properties of decimals

1 all three lines are the same length
(a) = = (b) end unchanged **2** 3.90,
300.00, 1.400 10.005, 0.103, 100,
20.002 **3** (a) 600.06 (b) 3.5 (c) 700
(d) 13.9 (e) 303.33 (f) 10.1
4 (a) 1.400 (b) 5.040 (c) 8.000
(d) 30.400 (e) 9.400 (f) 10.000
5 (a) < (b) > (c) = (d) >
(e) = (f) = (g) < (h) = (i) =
(j) < **6** (a) C (b) C (c) D (d) B
(e) C **7** 0.6 0.600 37.0 37.00
37.000 19.9 19.90 **8** $\frac{1}{1000}$ < 0.1021 <
0.112 < 0.120 < 1.1 **9** C = 0.03 B is a pure decimal with three decimal places between 0.021 ~ 0.028. D is a pure decimal with three decimal places between 0.022 ~ 0.029.

Unit test 6

1 (a) 0.29 zero point two nine two pure 29 0.71 (b) third second
(c) 0.57 (d) 94 (e) 0 3 7 (f) 1.2
mixed 1 2 (g) ones ones thousandths
thousandths (h) 1000 $\frac{1}{10}$ (i) 10.99
(j) 200.02 hundredths 200.020
2 (a) 0.25 (b) 0.5 (c) 0.75 (d) 0.1
(e) 0.17 (f) 0.999 **3** (a) $\frac{3}{10}$ (b) $\frac{1}{4}$
(c) $\frac{7}{100}$ (d) $\frac{21}{100}$ (e) $\frac{3}{4}$ (f) $\frac{191}{1000}$
4

Decimal numbers	Can some zeros be dropped off without changing its value? (Yes or No)	If the answer is yes, write the number after dropping the zeros
0.7040	Yes	0.704
7.000	Yes	7

(continued)

Decimal numbers	Can some zeros be dropped off without changing its value? (Yes or No)	If the answer is yes, write the number after dropping the zeros
68.0100	Yes	68.01
200.060	Yes	200.06
0.007	No	N/A
230.0900	Yes	230.09

5 (a) D (b) B (c) A (d) D
6 (a) × (b) × (c) × (d) √
(e) × **7** (a) 0.36 (b) 0.04
(c) 110.00 (d) 1.60 or 1.6 (e) 3.04
(f) 0.90 or 0.9 **8** (a) 0.550 0.505
0.5 0.055 (b) 0.0054 km < 5 km 4 m <
5.04 km < 5.40 km **9** 16 0 10 120
10 (a) 0.135, 0.153, 0.315, 0.351, 0.513,
0.531 (b) 5.013, 5.031, 5.103, 5.301,
5.130, 5.310 (c) 10.35, 10.53, 30.15,
30.51, 50.13, 50.31 **11** James

Chapter 7 Statistics (Ⅲ)

7.1 Knowing line graphs (1)

1 (a) time temperature 0.5 degrees
Celsius (b) at 08:00 40℃ (c) 2
(d) from 06:00 to 08:00 (e) from 10:00 to
12:00 (f) from 16:00 to 18:00 (g) She
was getting better. Her temperature showed
downward tendency from 8 o'clock in the
morning **2**

Time	06:00	08:00	10:00	12.00	14:00	16:00	18:00
Temperature (℃)	37.5	40	39.5	37.5	38	37	37

3 (a) at 08:00 and 17:00 the rush hour
because people go to work in the morning
and go back home in the afternoon (answer
may vary) (b) at 12 noon the volume of
people is the least during lunch time (c) answer
may vary

7.2 Knowing line graphs (2)

1 (a) month quantity sold (b) December
June 250 400 (c) June to December
January to June (d) July January 250
350 (e) January to July July to December
(f) from the highest point of each graph and
taking into account of the change of
seasons, picnic blankets have the highest
sales volume in summer while wool quilts
have the lowest volume **2** (a) line bar
(b) C A (c) 9:30 downward
(d) 11:30 14:00 9:30 11:30

7.3 Knowing line graphs (3)

1 (a) D C (b) B (c) A **2** (a) 100
marks, 70 marks (b) it means the blank
part. (c) from unit test 5 (d) unit test 4
(e) Adams's scores mostly improve (f)

Unit	One	Two	Three	Four	Five	Six	Seven	Eight
Scores	70	77	75	90	85	95	98	100

(g) Adam appears to have studied for all but
tests 3 and 5; he steadily improved (answers
may vary) (h) answers may vary

7.4 Constructing line graphs

1 (b) unit (c) axes **2** graph showing
Monday – Sunday on the horizontal axis, 0 –
50 on the vertical axis, the points correctly
plotted and straight lines connecting the points
(a) Wednesday 46 people (b) Saturday
and Sunday (c) The first half of the week
shows an increasing tendency, while the
second half of the week shows a downward
trend. (answer may vary) (d) 244
3 (a) bar chart showing the same axes as
before, with bars correctly drawn
(b) answer may vary **4** answer may vary

Unit test 7

1 500 4 50 2400 190 350 1 60
2 (a) 4116 (b) 7248 (c) 3156(3156 ÷
4 = 789) (d) 9 (e) 22 (f) 112 r 3
(112 × 70 + 3 = 7843) **3** 913 1559
17 000 **4** (a) D C A B (b) (i) 5
35 (ii) 5 (iii) 4 (iv) 1 5 (v) 110
5 (a) B (b) E **6** (a) the 12th 18

pupils （b）the 10th and 11th （c）the 13th, 15th, 16th and 17th （d）The tendency of line graphs shows the number of absentees will likely continue to fall. （answer may vary） （e）103 **7** （a）

Year group	Year 1	Year 2	Year 3	Year 4	Year 5
Number of books donated	50	65	85	150	230

（b）graph showing Year 1 – Year 5 on the horizontal axis, 0 – 250 on the vertical axis, the points correctly plotted and straight lines connecting the points （c）It shows a tendency to increase with successive year groups. （answer may vary） （d）bar chart showing the same axes as before, with bars correctly drawn （e）580 books

Chapter 8 Geometry and measurement (Ⅰ)

8.1 Acute and obtuse angles

1 obtuse obtuse acute right
2 acute angles: half past 3 half past 5 11 o'clock right angles: 3 o'clock 9 o'clock obtuse angles: 4 o'clock half past 9 **3** 6 4 4 8 **4** （a）× （b）√ （c）× （d）× **5** acute angles: ①④⑦ right angles: ③⑥ obtuse angles: ②⑤⑧ **6** 5 16 **7** +

8.2 Triangles and quadrilaterals (1)

1 triangles: ③⑦⑨⑩⑬ quadrilaterals: ① ②④⑤⑧⑪⑫⑭⑮ **2** the three shapes correctly copied on the grid **3** （a）3 square （b）3 3 4 4 （c）quadrilaterals opposite four （d）square （e）5 1 **4** （a）× （b）× （c）√ （d）× **5** answers may vary
（a）

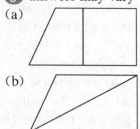

（b）

（c）

6 8 10

8.3 Triangles and quadrilaterals (2)

1 hexagon quadrilateral triangle quadrilateral rectangle pentagon octagon square **2** （a）√ （b）√ （c）× （d）√ **3** （a）dots connected to form a triangle around the puppy, a quadrilateral around the monkey and a rectangle around the zebra （b）triangle quadrilateral rectangle （c）baby zebra **4** （a）②⑤⑦⑨⑪⑯ （b）②③⑤⑧⑩⑪⑬ ⑯ （c）⑭⑮ **5**

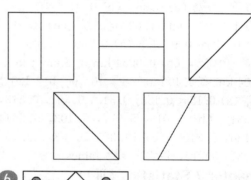

6

8.4 Classification of triangles (1)

1 （a）right-angled triangle ② ⑤ ⑩ （b）obtuse angle ⑦ ⑧ （c）acute angle acute-angled triangle ③④⑥⑨ **2** obtuse-angled right-angled acute-angled **3** （a）√ （b）× （c）× （d）× **4** triangles correctly drawn as described **5**

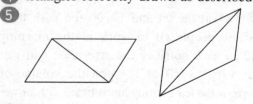

6 6 or 5 or 4

8.5 Classification of triangles (2)

1 acute-angled triangles: ②⑤⑥ right-angled triangles: ①⑦ obtuse-angled triangles: ③④ **2** (a) B (b) B (c) D (d) D (e) B (f) D **3** 13 5 6 2

4 (a)

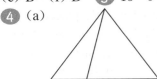

(b)   (c)

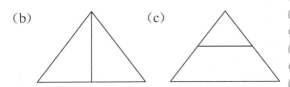

(answers may vary)

5

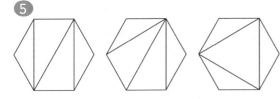

8.6 Line symmetry

1 √ √ × √ × **2** a line of symmetry drawn on the first, second and fourth shapes **3** 0, 3, 8, with lines of symmetry drawn **4** symmetrical shapes completed on the grids **5** A, B, C, D, E, H, I, K, M, O, T, U, V, W, X, Y, with lines of symmetry drawn **6** (a), (b) symmetrical shapes completed on the grids

8.7 Classification of triangles (3)

1 (a) isosceles (b) equilateral (c) symmetry 1 (d) symmetry 3 (e) special (f) acute-angled **2** (a) ①③ ⑤⑩ (b) ②④⑧ (c) ⑥⑦⑨ (d) ①②⑤ ⑦⑨⑩ (e) ⑤ **3** triangles correctly drawn with lines of symmetry shown

4 (a)   (b)

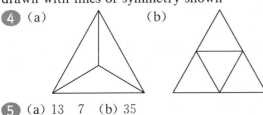

5 (a) 13 7 (b) 35

8.8 Areas

1 9 9 11 11 **2** 20 20 18 19 12 12 2 112 **3** 16 13 42 **4** any three shapes drawn with areas 7, 9 and 12 squares respectively **5** 3 5.5

8.9 Areas of rectangles and squares (1)

1 (a) 16 cm² 4 × 4 = 16(cm²) side × side (b) 15 cm² 3 × 5 = 15(cm²) length × width **2** (a) 24 cm² (b) 24 cm² (c) 25 cm² **3** 405 cm² **4** 1200 cm² **5** 1250 m² **6** 3 combinations, they are: 1×12, 2×6, 3×4 **7** 144 cm²

8.10 Areas of rectangles and squares (2)

1 (a) 12 cm² (b) 36 cm² (c) 7 cm **2** 9450 cm² **3** 144 cm² **4** 160 cm² **5** 1200 cm² **6** 280 cm²

8.11 Square metres

1 1 square metre 1 m² 1 square centimetre 1 cm² **2** m² cm² m² cm² m cm² m² m² **3** 40 m² 2500 m² 18 m **4** 2400 m² **5** 400 cm² **6** 5000 kg **7** 176 m² **8** 640 m²

Unit test 8

1 (a) ②⑤ (b) acute angles ①③⑧ (c) obtuse angles ④⑥⑦ **2** (a) triangles: ⑥⑦⑨⑪⑬ acute-angled triangles: ⑥⑪ right-angled triangles: ⑦⑨ obtuse-angled triangles: ⑬ (b) quadrilaterals: ②③④⑤ ⑩⑫ rectangle: ③⑩ square: ⑩ (c) ①⑧ **3** B **4** D C **5** D **6** answers may vary, for example:

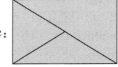

7 (a) 1 m 1 m² (b) cm m² (c) 600 cm² (d) equilateral triangle (e) 4 2 **8** (a) A C D (b) E (c) D (d) B F **9** (a) √ (b) × (c) × **10** (a) D (b) B (c) B **11** (a) 180 m² (b) 81 m² **12** Both are isosceles triangles. Each has one line of symmetry, drawn from the vertex where the two equal sides meet. **13** 9 cm² 13.5 cm² **14** (a) 4140 cm² (b) 300 000 cm² or 30 m² (c) 1200 cm² (d) 256 m²

Chapter 9   Geometry and measurement (II)

9. 1   Converting between kilometres and metres

1 (a) 8000   (b) 1600   (c) 100   (d) 0.7 (e) 4   (f) 470   (g) 5250   (h) 4026   (i) 9 (j) 1780   (k) 16 000   (l) 500   **2** (a) km (b) m   (c) km   (d) m   (e) km   **3** (a) > (b) <   (c) <   (d) =   (e) >   (f) > (g) <   (h) <   **4** (a) 5454 m > 5 km > 4545 m > 4 km   (b) 20 220 m > 20 202 m > 10 000 m > 9 km   **5** (a) 3000 m   (b) 292 m 6332 m   **6** (a) 14 000 m per minute, 233.3 m per second   (b) 18 km per hour

9. 2   Perimeters of rectangles and squares (1)

1 (a) 40 cm   (b) 22 cm   **2** (a) 74 cm 210 cm² 180 cm 2000 cm² 14 m 6 m² (b) 60 cm 225 cm² 12 m 144 m² **3** 90 m 200 m²   **4** 100 m   **5** 150 m **6** 550 cm², 1650 cm²   **7** 6 combinations 1+11, 2+10, 3+9, 4+8, 5+7, 6+6 No, when the perimeters of rectangles are equal, the nearer the length and width are to being equal, the greater the area will be.

9. 3   Perimeters of rectangles and squares (2)

1 92 m 68 cm   **2** (a) 150 cm 13 500 cm² 23 cm 84 cm 50 m 144 m²   (b) 96 cm 576 cm² 25 cm 625 cm²   **3** 96 cm, 320 cm²   **4** 110 m   **5** 17 cm   **6** (a) 2 combinations   (b) 108 cm 72 cm   **7** big square: 60 cm 225 cm² small square: 20 cm 25 cm² remaining paper: 30 cm 50 cm²

9. 4   Perimeters and areas of rectilinear shapes

1 (a) 24 cm 20 cm²   (b) 24 cm 24 cm² (c) 32 cm 28 cm²   (d) 28 cm 24 cm² **2** (a) 1000 cm², 200 cm   (b) 850 cm², 150 cm   **3** 242 cm²   **4** 729 m² **5** 36 cm²   **6** (a) 198 cm²   (b) 72 cm **7** 8500 cm²   **8** 144 cm²

9. 5   Describing positions on a 2-D grid

1 lines drawn from Tom to seat 6 in the second row from the bottom (screen) and from Joan to seat 3 in the top row.

2 horizontally   vertically   **3** Tiger (3, 3)   Rabbit (5, 4)   Horse (5, 2)   Sheep (7, 3)   Monkey (8, 5)   Cat (9, 1)   Dog (10, 2)   **4** marks correctly placed in the grid   **5** (a) (4, 5)   (b) answer may vary, for example, it can move 4 squares down, and then move 2 squares right. **6** (a) 9   1   (b) 495

9. 6   Solving problems involving time and money (1)

1 (a) 12   (b) 365   366   (c) 28   29 (d) 90 days in a common year (for example 2015).   **2** (a) 60   3600   (b) 90   (c) 45 2700   (d) $\frac{3}{4}$ (e) 3   10   (f) 60   (g) 21 504   (h) 6   **3** 9:09 a.m. or 9:09 p.m. 09:09   21:09   4:28 p.m.   16:28   1:24 a. m. or 1:24 p.m.   01:24 or 13:24   11:31 p.m.   23:31   **4** 20:45   **5** (a) 13   91 (b) £1235   £8645   (c) £364   £2548 **6** 2   24   **7** (a) 15 × 181 = 2715 (kWh) (answer may vary)   (b) 12 × 15 = 180p = £1.80   12 × 15 × 181 = 32 580 p = £325.80

9. 7   Solving problems involving time and money (2)

1 (a) 100   (b) 10   (c) 0.6   (d) 75 (e) 8   90   (f) 0.01   (g) 8050   (h) 238 **2** (a) 6   (b) 3   (c) 648   **3** 12 × 4 + 4 × 75 = 348 (pounds)   **4** (a) 2512 × 12 = 30 144 (pounds)   (b) 9.5 × 8 × 5 = 380 (pounds); estimation may vary.   (c) more than half of Emily's salary.   **5** (a) £258 £1806   (b) £1806   **6** 6 × 80 × 0.99 = 475.20 (pounds)   **7** 15 × 30 × 14 = 6300 (pounds)   6500 − 6300 = 200 (pounds) Yes, the budget is £200 more than the total purchase price.

Unit test 9

1 (a) 90   (b) 3   500   (c) 1.6   (d) km (e) the side length   (f) the length   the width   (g) 12   720   (h) 2.5   2   50 **2** (a) 3.6   360   (b) 320 cm   (c) 20 m 18 m²   **3** (a) 32 m   50 cm   12 cm

(b) 96 m   6 m   360 cm   **4** (a) ✗
(b) ✗   (c) ✗   (d) √   **5** 52 cm   88 cm^2
6 (8, 5)   **7** (a) 6300 m   6.3 km
(b) 625 cm^2 (c) 300 m^2 (d) 876 m^2
(e) 400 cm^2 784 cm^2 (f)(i) £69
(ii) £71   (g)(i) 84   (ii) £175   £2100
8 (i) 420   (ii) 5040p， £50.40

Chapter 10   Four operations of whole numbers

10.1   Calculating work efficiency (1)

1 Mr. Edge was the fastest.   Compare their work efficiencies.   **2** (a) ÷
(b) ✗   time taken   (c) ÷   work efficiency
3 (a) $132 ÷ 4 = 33$ (pages)   (b) $32 × 5 = 160$ (mental sums)   (c) $480 ÷ 30 = 16$ (hours)   (d) $270 ÷ 3 = 90$ $400 ÷ 5 = 80$
Adam has higher work efficiency   **4** $144 ÷ (216 ÷ 3) = 2$ (minutes)   **5** $1200 ÷ 30 - 1200 ÷ 40 = 10$ (metres)

10.2   Calculating work efficiency (2)

1 (a) $1000 ÷ 50 = 20$ (hours) They need 20 hours to make 1000 paper cranes.   (3) $288 ÷ 6 = 48$ (paper cranes) They made 48 paper cranes every hour on average.   **2** (a) $(18 + 4) × 22 = 484$ (kilowatts)   (b) $18 ÷ 3 = 6$ (bags) $14 ÷ 2 = 7$ (bags) $20 ÷ 4 = 5$ (bags)
Cathy made the most bags per hour.
(c) $(6480 ÷ 8) + 6480 = 7290$ (pieces)
3 (a) $9600 ÷ 4 = 2400$ (books)   (b) $9600 ÷ (4 × 30) = 80$ (books)   (c) $9600 ÷ 20 = 480$ (books)   (d) $9600 ÷ (4 × 30 × 20) = 4$ (books)

10.3   Solving calculation questions in 3 steps (1)

1 (a) 20   (b) 24   (c) 16   (c) 27
2 (a) 24   (b) 14   (c) 15   (d) 13   (e) 3
(f) 24   (g) 13   (h) 24   (i) 1   **3** (a) $(6 - 5 + 2) × 8 = 24$ (b) $[8 - (11 - 9)] × 4 = 24$ $(11 - 4) + 8 + 9 = 24$(answers may vary)
4 (a) $4 × 2 × (6 - 3) = 24$ (b) $3 × (6 + 4 - 2) = 24$ (c) $3 × 6 + 2 + 4 = 24$ (d) $2 × 6 + 3 × 4 = 24$ (answers may vary)
5 (a) $(7 × 7 - 1) ÷ 2 = 24$ (b) $6 + (2 ×$

$7) + 4 = 24$ (c) $12 × [4 - (8 - 6)] = 24$ (d) $(13 - 1) × (12 - 10) = 24$ (answers may vary)   **6** (a) √   (b) √   (c) ✗
(d) ✗   (e) √   **7** (a) $6 × (9 - 8) = 6$ (b) $(4 + 6) ÷ 2 = 5$ (c) $6 ÷ 3 + 1 = 3$ (d) $3 × 5 + 1 = 16$ (e) $3 × 8 - 15 = 9$ (f) $2 × (7 - 2) = 10$

10.4   Solving calculation questions in 3 steps (2)

1 (b) $182 ÷ (28 - 14) = 13$ (c) $(128 + 72) ÷ (20 × 5) = 2$ **2** (a) D   (b) B
3 (a) $650 ÷ 50 + 45 + 60 = 118$ (b) $35 × 6 - 121 ÷ 11 = 199$ **4** (a) 157   (b) 58
(c) 1067   (d) 1217   **5** $142 ÷ 2 - 7 × 9 + 2 = 10$ **6** $(120 + 20) ÷ 2 = 70$(cm)

10.5   Solving calculation questions in 3 steps (3)

1 (a) $(45 - 20) + 650 ÷ 50 = 38$ (b) $(121 + 11) ÷ (35 - 23) = 11$ **2** (a) 48   (b) 246
(c) 4   (d) 6120   (e) 66   (f) 194
3 (a) multiplication and division   addition and subtraction   (b) the calculation in the bracket   (c) multiplication   subtraction   division   **4** (a) $(42 + 567) ÷ 40 = 15$ (coaches) r 9 (pupils) $15 + 1 = 16$ (coaches)
(b) (i) $360 ÷ (34 - 22) = 30$ (kilograms)
(ii) $360 ÷ (34 - 22) × (34 + 22) = 1680$ (kilograms)   (iii) $(34 + 22) × 80 = 4480$ (pounds)   **5** $(480 - 360) ÷ (12 + 8) = 6$ $480 - 360 ÷ (12 + 8) = 462$ **6** $(724 - 88) ÷ 2 ÷ 3 = 106$ (books)

10.6   Solving calculation questions in 3 steps (4)

1 $27 × [2520 ÷ (37 + 53)] = 756$
2 (a) $660 ÷ [(247 - 82) × 2] = 2$
(2) $[1000 - (70 + 20)] × 2 = 1820$
3 (a) round brackets   square brackets
20   (b) division   multiplication
(c) division   addition   subtraction
multiplication   (d) 77   (e) 1999.45
4 (a) 33   (b) 41   (c) 40   (d) 3004
(e) 75   (f) 27   **5** (a) $21 - (21 - 15) × 3 = 3$ (kilograms)

10.7   Working forward

1 $(24 ÷ 3 + 14) × 9 = 198$ **2** (a) 200

82 164 $(1000 \div 5 - 118) \times 2 = 164$
(b) 393 24 3 $(1285 - 892 - 369) \div 8 = 3$
3 (a) $(17 + 2) \times 2 - 2 = 36$ (b) $(71 - 15 \times 2) \times 24 = 984$ **4** (a) $12 - 2 + 6 - 3 + 4 = 17$ (passengers) (b) $360 \times 3 + 32 = 1112$ (chickens) **5** $(68 \div 2 + 8) \div 3 = 14$ (years old) **6** 11 times

10. 8 Working backward
1 $(72 \div 8 - 8) \times 8 = 8$ **2** (a) 79
113 339 $(149 + 190) \div 3 - 34 = 79$
(b) 2093 91 15 $(750 \div 50 + 76) \times 23 = 2093$ **3** (a) $160 \div 8 - 8 = 12$ (b) $(45 \times 8 - 20) \div 5 = 68$ **4** (a) $(100 \div 20 + 14) \times 3 - 4 = 53$ (years old) (b) $(7 \times 7 - 7) \div 7 + 7 = 13$ (pomegranates) **5** $(48 + 24) \times 5 \div 8 = 45$ **6** $[(13 + 5) \times 2 + 6] \times 2 = 84$ (pages)

10. 9 Word calculation problems (1)
1 (a) Product = quotient $\times 12$ $150 \div 6 \times 12 = 300$ (b) Quotient = sum $\div 30$ $(288 + 42) \div 30 = 11$ **2** (a) C (b) B (c) A
(d) D **3** (a) $600 \div 20 + 187 = 217$
(b) $500 \times 32 \div 100 = 160$ (c) $470 \times 15 - 17 \times 104 = 5282$ (d) $244 \div (244 \div 2 - 118) = 61$ (e) $1098 - 756 \div 2 = 720$ **4** $820 \times 208 = 170\,560$ **5** $(37 - 9) \div (3 - 1) = 14$ (years old)

10. 10 Word calculation problems (2)
1 (a) product = quotient $\times$ difference
$210 \div 7 \times (120 - 80) = 1200$ (b) sum = product + quotient $34 \times 12 + 48 \div 12 = 412$
2 (a) $(66 \times 25) \div (6 \times 5) = 55$ (b) $2940 - 2940 \div 20 = 2793$ (c) $128 \times 50 + 36 = 6436$ (d) $2 \times 72 - 6300 \div 60 = 39$
3 (a) C (b) A (c) D (d) B
4 (a) the difference between the product of 403 multiplied by the difference of 213 subtracted by 90 and 13.495 56 (b) the quotient of 864 divided by the quotient of the difference between 2193 and 1473 divided by 90.108 **5** $(1000 - 456) \div 4 = 136$

10. 11 Laws of operations (1)
1 (a) order unchanged $b + a$ (b) order unchanged $b \times a$ (c) unchanged $b + c$

(d) unchanged $b \times c$ **2** (a) 732 (b) 621
248 (c) 14 (d) 250 4 (e) ☆ △
(6) ◇ ◎ (f) y z (8) k l
3 (a) 2575 (b) 1543 (c) 8151
(d) 34 983 **4** (a) 669 (b) 1123
(c) 7500 (d) 3400 (e) 1310 (f) 91 000
5 (a) 600 (b) 12 000 (c) 1 111 110

10. 12 Laws of operations (2)
1 (a) 80 (b) 25 (c) 44 56 (d) b a
(e) b c (f) b c (g) 33 84
(h) ■ ▲ (i) 75 2 8 125
2 (a) 300 (b) 100 000 (c) 1600
(d) 54 000 (e) 11 000 (f) 700 000
3 (a) $(6 \times 4) \times 25 = 600$ (pounds) or $6 \times (4 \times 25) = 600$ (pounds) (b) $40 \div 5 \div 4 = 2$ (pounds) or $40 \div 4 \div 5 = 2$ (pounds) or $40 \div (5 \times 4) = 2$ (pounds) (c) $2 \times (8 \times 25) = 400$ (flowers) or $(2 \times 8) \times 25 = 400$ (flowers)
4 (a) 320 000 (b) 7

10. 13 Laws of operations (3)
1 (a) C (b) B (c) A (d) answer may vary (e) $a \times (b + c) = a \times b + a \times c$
2 (a) 64 49 $+$ (b) □ $\times$ (c) 15
42 35 (d) $-$ a d (e) $55 \times (22 - 11)$
(f) $+$ 73 **3** (a) $\times$ (b) $\times$ (c) $\sqrt{}$
(d) $\times$ (e) $\sqrt{}$ (f) $\sqrt{}$ **4** (a) 7800
(b) 2400 (c) 180 (d) 7600 (e) 3192
(f) 4500 (g) 4257 (h) 20 907 **5** 150
(Hint: $50 \times 4 - 50 = 150$)

10. 14 Laws of operations (4)
1 (a) commutative law of addition and associative law of addition (b) associative law of multiplication (c) distributive law of multiplication over addition (d) distributive law of multiplication over subtraction.
2 (a) 1200 (b) 8000 (c) 19 899
3 (a) 5959 (b) 3500 (c) 1200 (d) 2100
(e) 37 500 (f) 100 000 **4** (a) $12 \times 32 + 12 \times 18 = 600$ (passengers) (b) $(30 + 4) \times 25 = 850$ (kilograms) **5** (a) 36 000
(b) 1 000 000

10. 15 Problem solving using four operations (1)
1 (a) $1200 \div 40 = 30$ (metres per day)
(b) $30 + 10 = 40$ (metres per day)

(c) $1200 \div 40 = 30$ (days) **2** (a) $91 \times 10 \div 7 = 130$ (metres) $91 \times 10 \div 7 - 91 = 39$ (metres)   (b) $81 \times 10 \div (81 + 9) = 9$ (days) $10 - 9 = 1$ (day)   (3) $360 \div 60 - 360 \div 90 = 2$ (days)   (4) $360 \div 4 - 360 \div 6 = 30$ (pages) (5) $3000 \div 20 - 3000 \div 30 = 50$ (kilograms) (6) $135 \div 3 - 126 \div 3 = 3$ (kicks)

3 $3600 \div (3600 \div 30 + 3600 \div 20) = 12$ (days) **4** $(25 \times 15 - 25 \times 3) \div 10 - 25 = 5$ (people)

10.16 Problem solving using four operations (2)

1 (a) B (b) A **2** (a) Method 1: $(1620 - 60 \times 9) \div 60 = 18$ (days)   Method 2: $1620 \div 60 - 9 = 18$ (days)   (b) Method 1: $56 \div 4 \times 8 = 112$ (toys)   Method 2: $56 \times (8 \div 4) = 112$ (toys)   **3** (a) $(460 - 120) \div (120 \div 6) = 17$ (days)   (b) $82\,800 - (82\,800 \div 60 \times 44) = 22\,080$ (square metres)   (3) $(4920 - 2400) \div (2400 \div 20) = 21$ (days)   (4) $600 \div 8 \div (100 \div 5 \div 4) = 15$ (workers)   **4** 37 637

5 price of a chair: $2400 \div (20 \times 3 + 40) = 24$ (pounds); price of a desk: $24 \times 3 = 72$ (pounds)

10.17 Problem solving using four operations (3)

1 (a) $10 \times (16 \div 8) = 20$ (pounds)   (b) $36 \times (270 \div 10) = 972$ (pounds)   (c) $2 \times (12 \div 3) + 3 \times (25 \div 5) = 23$ (pounds)   (d) $2 \times (12 \div 3) + 4 \times (16 \div 8) = 16$ (pounds)

2 (a) $(120 \div 8) \times 24 + 120 = 480$ (computers) (b) $(680 - 65 \times 4) \div 6 = 70$ (pieces) (c) $240 + (240 \times 2) + 8 = 728$ (kilometres) (d) $(150 + 50) \times 3 - 20 = 580$ (trees)

3 120 **4** Mum: $(78 - 11 + 2) \div 3 = 23$ (oranges)   Dad: $23 + 11 = 34$ (oranges) Ben: $23 - 2 = 21$ (oranges)

10.18 Problem solving using four operations (4)

1 6 pens **2** $600 \div (160 \div 8) = 30$ (minutes) **3** $126 + 12 \times (126 \div 9) = 294$ (tiles) **4** $100\,000 \div 2 \div (75\,000 \div 3 \div 5) = 10$ (lorries) **5** $(255 - 37 \times 5) \div 2 = 35$ (pages) **6** $(900 \div 30 - 5) \times 25 = 625$ (kilograms) **7** $(7 \times 60) \times (60 \div 30) = 840$ (kilometres) **8** The number of sweaters in each cardboard box: $480 \div (2 \times 2 + 8) = 40$ (sweaters) the number of sweaters in each plastic box: $40 \times 2 = 80$ (sweaters)

9 One plate: $(87 - 39) \div (6 - 2) = 12$ (pounds) One bowl: $(87 - 12 \times 6) \div 3 = 5$ (pounds) or $(39 - 12 \times 2) \div 3 = 5$ (pounds) **10** Child B: $(108 + 18 - 12) \div 3 = 38$ (pictures) Child A: $38 - 18 = 20$ (pictures) Child C: $38 + 12 = 50$ (pictures)

Unit test 10

1 120   100   1000   50   1   162   101 800   7000 **2** (a) 125 460   (b) 4389 **3** (a) 2500   (b) 50 500   (c) 4092 (d) 9000   (e) 880 000   (f) 101 000 (g) 640   (h) 1800 **4** (a) commutative law of multiplication and associative law of multiplication   (b) commutative law of addition   (c) $(\blacklozenge + \bullet) \times \bigstar$ (d) 84 33 (e) 27   18   (f) 9001   (g) 46   (h) 1 (i) 10   (j) 19   (k) 63   (l) 4500 (m) greater than   (n) amount of work time taken **5** (a) $\times$ (b) $\times$ (c) $\checkmark$ (d) $\checkmark$ **6** (a) $[(240 \div 20) + 79] \times 36 = 3276$ (b) $[(144 \times 5) + 250] \times 10 = 9700$

7 (a) $(1100 - 2) \div 18 = 61$ (b) $840 \div (129 - 59) \times 66 = 792$ (c) $(19 - 5) \div 7 + 3 = 5$ **8** (a) $(720 - 240) \div (240 \div 3) = 6$ (hours)   (b) $120 \div (120 \div 12 - 2) = 15$ (containers)   (c) $60 \times 110 \div 100 - 60 = 6$ (sets)   (d) $(1125 - 185) \div 20 = 47$ (kilograms)

End of year test

1 99   3500   144   30   40   391   200 6000   0   4239   21   120 **2** 5474 39 232   7001 **3** 9500   5600   880   1 $\frac{5}{8}$ 0 **4** (a) $201 \times 37 + 17 = 7454$

(b) $18 \times 45 - 36 = 774$ **5** (a) 0.48 (b) 45   (c) 25   350   25 350   (d) $10\,000 > 9908 > 9889 > 8957 > 7999$ 9889   (e) 9 (f) 6   (g) $\frac{91}{100}$ (h) 25   (i) 2   0   4   (j) 3 (k) 3   (l) 4   16   (m) 66   94 **6** (a) $\checkmark$ (b) $\times$ (c) $\checkmark$ (d) $\times$ (e) $\times$ **7** (a) B (b) A   (c) C   (d) B   (e) C

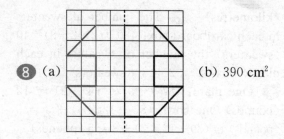

8 (a) (b) 390 cm²

9 (a) 6 (b) 684 pages (c) (i) 30 m
(ii) 825 m² (d) £525 (e) (i) line
(ii) June, November (iii) April May,
October November (iv) 92